Tales of the Deep State

Preface:

For over thirty years a gang of wealthy global influence peddlers and embedded bureaucrats have manipulated much of government, finance, and media. Behind the scenes, members of this so-called Deep State have pulled the strings on important economic, social, and political decisions.

Challenging the Deep State is dangerous, careers have been ruined, people have been found dead or just disappear.

These tales expose the Deep State and the growing threat it represents to the average American's liberty, happiness, and life.

Copyright@ Mike Hourston
This is a work of fiction. Names, characters, and incidents depicted in these stories are products of the author's imagination and are used fictitiously. Any resemblance to actual events, or persons living or dead, is entirely coincidental and beyond the intent of the author.

Tales of the Deep State

CONTENTS

The Weeping Willow Mystery

"No one escapes the wrath of the Deep State"

It began when Clifford Hogan said, "I was lying under a weeping willow tree and God told me that He intervened in the last presidential election."

The army veteran's statement lit a fire across social media; there was ridicule and rants countered by emotional and spiritual support. Liar, dumb, stupid, and crazy were main stream media's dismissive words for Hogan and those who accepted his claim.

The *Journal*, a respected New York paper with a three-hundred thousand daily circulation, sent investigative reporter Nick Cyrus to Utopia, Tennessee to get the story.

Fifty-seven, gray haired, and overweight, Nick was a ten-year veteran of the *Journal*. He shared a small brownstone in Greenwich Village with a fifteen-year old black and white cat named Beau. He attended church at Saint Joseph's on East 8th Street, and volunteered at their food bank. Nick's son lived in the Chicago area, but he hadn't heard from him in over ten years. Crime and politics was his beat, but as the only reporter at the *Journal* with religious affiliation Nick also got the God stories to investigate.

Nick hugged Beau goodbye that Saturday in mid-May, left him with a neighbor, and then headed to JFK Airport. Most of his colleagues thought this was a joke assignment, but Nick sensed Utopia held an important story.

Monday in Utopia

Sunshine peeked through the dense oaks lining the two lane blacktop, as Nick drove to Utopia and answers. Located forty miles from Johnson City, buried deep in rural Tennessee, this outpost had become a chapter in a Washington political storm that had run non-stop since the election.

The FBI, Senate investigators, and people from Special Prosecutor Miller's staff had arrived on Sunday. Through traffic was diverted and a one-mile perimeter kept out sightseers while Hogan and others from the community were questioned. The site where the alleged message was delivered—under a weeping willow tree—had been scrubbed by a forensic team.

At six-thirty, Nick pulled up to the FBI barricade, flashed his press credentials, and said, "I didn't expect to find you guys here."

They demanded his cellphone and camera.

Nick stuck his head out the window. "No pictures? Are you guys serious?"

A tall bearded agent leaned against the wooden barricade and grinned. "Utopia is five minutes away. Do you want to get past or not? Your equipment will be returned."

"Ok, here you go. Careful with that camera, it cost a ton."

Nick reached Utopia, parked on the shoulder, and glanced around. There was a log cabin, next to it a craft store with gravel out front for a couple of cars. The other side of the road had an old livery stable and a wooden building with broken shingles and dilapidated roof. In front of the building children kicked a soccer ball around a grassy yard while a fat woman in a bright-yellow bathrobe smoked a cigarette and watched from the porch.

As Nick got out of the car two tan terriers ran up and barked and then took off in the direction of the log cabin. Down the road a few hundred feet two men and a woman were talking in front of a rusty mobile home. There it was; five old structures, twelve residents plus two dogs, surrounded by wilderness.

Nick approached a slender young lady sitting on the hood of a green sedan. "I'm with the *Journal*, and need to interview a fellow named Cliff Hogan."

She introduced herself as FBI agent Sanchez, and pointed at the mobile home. "He's the tall lanky, gray-haired guy in beat-up jeans. You better hurry; in two hours we haul him out of here and up to Washington for additional interrogation. Access will be difficult after that."

"You're taking Hogan to Washington? Do you think there's something to his story?"

Sanchez laughed. "No comment."

Nick watched the kids giggle and kick the soccer ball, and recalled how little you needed to have fun. The ball bounced over and Nick tapped it back in the direction of a perky little girl with a blue ribbon dangling from her blond hair. He remembered his baby sister had worn a ribbon just like that back in the day.

Nick approached the mobile home and hugged a long-ago girlfriend now working as a journalist at the *Johnson City Sentinel*, and then he introduced himself to Hogan and asked for an interview.

Hogan smiled. "Young man, I'd be glad to visit with you." He turned to the two *Sentinel* reporters, and said, "You folks can root around my trailer if you want."

Hogan grabbed Nick by the arm. "Let's go for a hike in the woods where we can think and experience stuff greater than us."

Glad he had worn tennis shoes and jeans; Nick jumped over a turtle and then sidestepped a baby rabbit—robins laughed and sang. Leafy tree branches dangled above while red and yellow wildflowers soaked the tight dusty path in a delicate perfume. Nick contrasted this with a morning stroll down Broadway with its exhaust fumes, fresh baked donut and corned beef smells, sirens and shouting citizens surrounded by fancy cut crystal, ornamental iron, and mountains of faded bricks.

The grass near the weeping willow tree was trampled. Nick sat down, and then glanced at a creek a few feet away; its water splashing over and around rocks in a hurry to get downstream.

Hogan stretched his thin frame under the weeping willow tree. "Yesterday, the boys from the FBI searched several hours around here. They bagged a bunch of stuff and hauled it out to a truck that left last night. They asked a lot of questions, even gave me a lie detector.

Everyone here has been questioned. I think they want to prove I'm a nut."

"Well, you claim God told you that He intervened in the last presidential election. In effect, He decided the winner. Is that correct?"

"You've got it."

"That's quite a story. Did He tell you why He picked sides in the election?"

"I reckon; He doesn't have to explain the how or why of His actions to me or anyone else."

Nick stared at Hogan. "How do you know this communication came from God?"

"A couple of weeks ago I was laying under this tree—just like now. It was quiet except for these nature sounds, and then this powerful voice—God's voice—announced from above what He had done in the presidential election. No lightning or thunder, but I knew it was Him. You can't mistake those things."

Nick watched an anxious rabbit grab a drink from the creek, and then turned to Hogan. "Did anyone else hear this voice? Have you heard this voice or other voices before?"

Hogan laughed. "No witnesses. No, I haven't heard this or any other voices before. The FBI boys asked me those same questions. And; no, I don't drink or take drugs. I guess a lot of folks have me pegged as a kook. That's OK, it is what it is."

"The folks in Utopia know you come out here to think. Maybe one of them rigged up a microphone or electronic recorder and pulled a fast one on you."

"Way out here in the woods? There isn't anyone around here with the skill or equipment to do that. Besides, I know them all for years. None of them would mess with God or me like that."

They watched a cardinal scrounge through the grass and a gray squirrel scamper up a nearby oak tree.

Hogan closed his eyes as a warm breeze shook the thin branches of the weeping willow. "This place teaches the importance of being humble. Tell them folks out East they're welcome to stop for a visit. They could reflect a little—maybe learn a little."

Nick nodded agreement. "A lot of people need to step down from their 'high ground' attitude. But don't expect them to change."

Hogan gazed at the sky. "Nick, the 'high ground' belongs to the Creator."

Nick stood, and said, "You don't seem like you'd have much to do with the Internet. How did this get out on social media so quick?"

"I'm seventy eight and never used a computer. The day after this happened I was at Sophie's craft shop when a couple from Indiana dropped in and asked directions. People never come to Utopia unless they're lost—except now of course. Anyway, they overheard me tell Sophie, a widow woman, what had happened under the weeping willow tree. The man tapped me on the shoulder and said he planned to share my story with the world. God works in mysterious ways. I guess He wanted this message out there."

Nick didn't know what to make of this old man's story. Hogan didn't appear to be lying. But people get confused; they hear and see stuff that isn't there. There weren't any witnesses. But, what did the FBI haul away to Washington?

Nick watched the cardinal circle overhead, and then said, "Cliff, this story has reached across America. People you never met hate you and others admire you. Do you feel like a prophet?"

"No, but I won't deny what happened. I'll go wherever God takes me on this."

Nick looked over at the creek. "How's the fishing?"

Hogan pointed, and said, "About a quarter mile the creek empties into a nice lake full of bass, crappie, and big catfish. We have that lake to ourselves. Don't know who owns it, never seen signs posted. I catch enough in a couple of hours to last me all week. Someday let's drop a line in there together."

"That's great, and you can teach me how to catch those big catfish."

Nick took a deep breath and leaned against the willow tree. "This place warms you up like an enchanting poem from Keats."

Hogan clapped, and said, "It's the oak and pine trees planted here at the beginning of time, spiced with the aroma of sweet flowers, soft summer winds, and the sound of fresh water breaking over ageless rocks. And then there are the birds and other gentle creatures that watch over this garden. It's poetry of rhythm and richness you won't experience anywhere else. Keats would love it here."

Nick smiled, and said, "If it's not too personal, how do you support yourself?"

Hogan laughed. "It doesn't take much. I paid five-hundred bucks for that Taj Mahal I live in. I retired from the army thirty years ago, that gets me a small pension. The rest comes from the land. I fish, scrounge nuts, seasonal fruits and berries. I get by—thank you.

"By the way, you need to get back here in early October. The rabbits, birds, and squirrels throw a fall festival and everyone is welcome. Last year a pair of condors flew all the way from California to attend."

Nick grinned. "Now that's something you won't find on Broadway. I'll try and check that out."

Nick thought Hogan was a bit eccentric, but he had a lot of gumption. He liked this skinny old veteran.

Around nine o'clock four husky men with FBI emblazed on their caps showed up. Hogan smiled as two of the men grabbed his thin arms and shuffled him back along the path. The other two spread yellow crime-scene tape around the weeping willow tree.

Nick waved as Hogan disappeared up the trail, and then walked over to the men near the tree. "You guys consider this the scene of a crime?"

One of them said, "No one is to get within fifty feet of this tree. We'll have people posted to make sure. That came straight from Washington."

Nick scratched his head. "Isn't that kind of strange?"

"We just follow orders."

Nick watched the men finish with the yellow tape, and then headed back to interview some of the other folks and learn more about Hogan, this tree, and other pieces that might help tie this together.

As Nick emerged from the woods a black sedan sped away with Hogan wedged between two men in the back seat. The door to Hogan's mobile home was closed and an armed guard posted in front of it. Nick's old girlfriend told him the FBI had chased the adults and their kids back inside their homes and told them not to give interviews.

Not even the dogs were around to bark. Nick wondered what lay in store for Hogan.

Wednesday in Washington

God's alleged role in the recent election was still a hot social media topic. Since Monday night Hogan had been held at a government safe house somewhere in the Washington area, while the bagged material from the weeping willow site was examined at FBI labs. A Wednesday morning press conference at the Dirksen Senate Office Building on Constitution Avenue had been called by Special Prosecutor Miller and Senator Jeannie Shoults who headed up the senate committee examining whether the recent presidential election had been tampered with.

When in Washington, Nick stayed at an old college friend's spacious red-brick townhouse in Georgetown. From there it was a cab ride to the senate office building.

Nick arrived at eight-fifteen and presented his press credentials. He entered a room with a deep-blue plush carpet and paneled walls stained a dark mahogany. At the front of the room was a large wooden table. Audience seating consisted of seventy-five metal folding chairs.

Nick grabbed a cup of coffee and waved at people from the *Post*, *Chronicle*, *Today*, and other media outlets bunched together on the other side of the room. He didn't think much of them or their journalism; they wrote alike, voted alike, hated alike, and let their agenda control facts in stories.

At nine o'clock Miller, with Shoults next to him, read a prepared statement.

"America's democracy depends on a free and fair election process. My task as Special Prosecutor has been to identify and prosecute those who tampered and manipulated processes in the recent Presidential election. So far the investigation has pointed in several directions, both domestic and foreign. The office of Special Prosecutor, the Senate Committee, and the FBI will study anything that may have played an improper role. The claim by Mr. Clifford Hogan has created anger, outrage, and disgust at the notion God

would take election sides. Others insist that God takes sides on all moral issues. Our job is to get to the truth of the matter, and that's what we intend to do."

Miller and Shoults sat down and invited questions.

The reporter from the *Chronicle* stood. "I'm Penny Worthington and want to know how you plan to expose this fake news?"

Miller cracked a smile, and said, "We've got the best investigators and tools in the world. They've examined this story since it broke a week ago. We'll go where the facts take us; our investigation will expose fairy tales."

Joe Carter, known as Fat Joe to his friends, raised his hand. "A lot of us think this whole God story is just a conspiracy to direct the investigation away from the focus on foreign involvement. Have you dropped that part of the investigation?"

Miller shook his head. "Don't worry, that's still our primary focus."

Carter threw his arms in the air, and said, "What have you learned so far about this God angle?"

Miller glanced over at Shoults, and then said, "For now, Clifford Hogan is sticking to his original claim. We also talked to other folks in Utopia."

Nick interrupted Miller. "What was all that material the FBI bagged and took back to Washington?"

Miller paused, and then said, "This is an active investigation, and we're not going to share what we've learned so far."

A young man dressed in jeans and bright-green sweatshirt raised his hand. "I'm Jason Sanders of *The Dispatch*, and my question is for Senator Shoults. How do you prove or disprove this? Besides Hogan, the only other witness would be God."

Senator Shoults leaned toward the microphone. "The Committee is prepared to do whatever is necessary to expose the truth. I've been hearing from a lot of constituents that want this issue debunked so we can get back to serious work. I also have to respond to those constituents that seem to accept Hogan's claims. I've discussed this with other committee members and we will force this issue to a head in the immediate future."

Nick wondered what Senator Shoults meant by "forcing the issue to a head." Would they make Hogan recant, or smear him with unnamed sources or leaks to receptive media outlets—use fake news to kill so-called fake news?

As Nick exited the conference, Carter rushed over and grabbed his arm. "Hey Nick, we're headed over to Barnacle's for lunch and a few cold ones, and we'd like you to come along."

"Not today, I have to meet someone back in Georgetown—maybe next time."

Nick relaxed at his friend's townhouse and sent his boss notes and comments on the press conference. He intended to find out where the FBI stashed Hogan and get a follow-up interview. Then, corner Senator Shoults and learn how she planned to force this issue to a head, which should generate a few juicy quotes. Plus, there was that material shipped from Utopia to Washington for analysis, a friend at the FBI might be able to help with that.

Nick chased his targets through the weekend. The FBI wouldn't reveal where they had taken Hogan. Nick spotted Senator Shoults at her favorite restaurant, but she refused to be interviewed. The Utopia material had gone through analysis at the FBI labs, but for once even his friend wouldn't talk. By Sunday night it was five days of dead ends.

Monday
Special Prosecutor Miller joined by Senator Shoults and her committee issued a subpoena that required God appear and give testimony before the senate committee at nine on Thursday.

They released a statement: *Mr. Clifford Hogan has made claims that involve God and the recent election process. This can only be cleared up by God Himself. Given His omnipresence, this announcement should be sufficient to alert Him, and we look forward to His appearance.*

Religious and a few others took offense at this announcement, but overall not many complaints. Nick figured this was a stunt, but the reason was unclear.

Monday night Nick dropped by Barnacle's, located on 19th Street in the Foggy Bottom area of Washington. Its white stone facade, massive cast iron doors, and stained glass windows were original to the fifty-thousand square-foot mansion built by a nineteenth-century steel baron. In earlier days it was used to wine and dine the wealthy and influential—a place to strike deals. With doormen dressed in navy-blue slacks and jackets with bright red ties, now it was the city's trendiest nightclub.

Barnacle's was where the town's A-listers, moneyed, and cultured savages fortified with booze, drugs, and attitude flattered each other while laughing at the less deserving. People referred to as journalists could always be found there. Nick would get their take on the announcement from the Special Prosecutor earlier in the day. Beltway rants could be an important part of the story.

Nick arrived at eight o'clock and ordered his favorite draught beer. He spotted a table packed with the usual gang from the *Post*, *Today*, and other media outlets.

Nick squeezed next to the *Times'* reporter, took a drink, and then yelled, "What do you guys think, will God show up Thursday?"

The *Times'* reporter slammed the table with his right hand, and then pointed in the air. "He will if He knows what's good for Him. Ignore a government subpoena and you'll get in a lot of trouble."

The reporter from the *Gazette* laughed. "Nobody is above the law, not even God."

Joe Carter from the *Post* asked, "How would He be sworn in? Would He swear an oath to Himself?" The table erupted in laughter.

In a slurred voice, Penny Worthington from the *Chronicle,* said, "He would have to touch the U.S. Constitution and give His oath to that. Of course, if He ignores the subpoena Miller and Shoults will have to issue a warrant for His arrest. We can't have people or spirits ignore the law."

It was sarcasm; Nick knew they didn't believe in God or anyone outside their special circle.

Nick waved his arms. "OK, you've made your points. But, why in the world or universe did those fools issue a subpoena like this? What's their motive?"

The *Times'* reporter leaned back in his chair, and said, "It's obvious, when the spirit fails to show it will put an end to this whole nutty episode and expose Hogan as a liar to those crazies out there that believe him. The Special Prosecutor and Senate Committee can then get back to serious work."

Nick said, "Alright, but they could have dealt with this in a more civil way. There are a lot of the faithful who don't believe you should put God to the test."

Nick stared at plates piled with half-eaten appetizers next to empty beer bottles. He figured a person's food and bar bill would be more here in one night than people in Utopia, Abilene, or anywhere in middle-America might spend on food in a month.

The *Times'* reporter elbowed Nick. "Hey Nick, I'll buy you another beer. I remember when you could drink everyone under the table."

"I've learned from my past, my limit is one these days."

"Come on, nobody pays out of their own pocket here or at any other restaurant around town. You know the game; these evenings always get thrown on the company card."

"Enjoy your business meeting. I'll see you guys at the senate office building on Thursday."

The *Times'* reporter nodded, and then ordered more appetizers and a fresh round of drinks.

Thursday

Storms and gusty winds shook the city all day. Nick's cab arrived as the rain picked up; he ran from the townhouse and jumped in for the ride to the senate building. At a stoplight near the metro station, Nick watched two scuffed up old women throw punches at each other in front of the Blue Moon Bar and Grill while a small crowd cheered from the doorway. On First Street the cab passed a shirtless old man sitting on a bench clutching a statue of a raven as rain pelted a green tarp thrown over his shoulders. Nick could get angry and weary, but nothing heaved up by this city ever shocked him.

Nick reached the Dirksen building around eight. Neither Miller nor Senator Shoults planned to appear; Miller had sent a young investigator named Harry Jones who was seated at a small wooden table in front.

The cramped, windowless room filled by eight-thirty—Nick recognized most. Religious condemned the event as disrespectful and blasphemous.

A throne chair and a name card marked GOD were placed on the other side of the table, directly opposite Jones. At eight-fifty, escorted by two FBI agents, Clifford Hogan in plaid shirt and jeans appeared and was seated to the left of Jones. The agents kept their eyes on Hogan from a few feet away.

Nick gazed at the old man he last saw ten days earlier. Hogan's flesh lacked color and hung on his face. There was a tremble in his right hand as he sat with his head lowered; the smile and energy were gone. Nick smacked his hands together in disgust.

At nine o'clock Jones announced the session would begin, and then looked at Hogan. "This person has made assertions about the past general election. The Special Prosecutor and Senate Committee chose to examine the issue because a portion of the public seemed to accept these ridiculous statements. Mr. Hogan continues to insist this communication from God occurred. We now call on God to come forward and confirm or refute Mr. Hogan's claim."

Jones pointed at the throne chair. "The subpoena has been issued; now let's see what happens." He took off his jacket, grabbed a cup of coffee and newspaper, and then sat down.

Five minutes of silence was followed by whispers, and then regular conversation took over.

Joe Carter of the *Post* turned to the reporter next to him. "What about lunch at that Chinese restaurant near the Mall?"

Sanders of the *Dispatch* laughed, and said, "Maybe someone should say hocus-pocus."

The *Guardian* reporter yelled, "I'll give it a few more minutes."

Nick noticed the *Times'* reporter, the one with unlimited expense vouchers, focused on his email messages. Fat Joe's fingers had turned orange from a bag of cheese puffs; the empty bag was shoved under his chair.

At nine twenty-five the reporter from the *Chronicle*, Penny Worthington, pointed at Hogan. "He makes me sick; it's time they got rid of him and those other fools out there." She grabbed her purse and knocked over a chair as she hurried out. Others followed.

At nine-thirty, FBI men took Hogan through a side door, and Jones announced the session ended.

Nick stared at the throne chair. This demonstration was meant to close down the story regardless of who was humiliated or abused along the way. Nick wanted to punch a lot of folks, but decided to get drunk instead. It was still raining as he left the building.

"God a No-Show" was the next day's tongue-in-cheek headline at the *Post*. The *Times* went further, "God Ignores Subpoena." Other stories implied that Hogan was under care at an asylum. One article suggested he confessed he made the story up. After a month America had moved on to the next big thing. And so it went another reality show whose season was over.

The ending didn't feel right to Nick. He pestered the FBI for the whereabouts of Hogan. An old source at the Bureau confirmed "off the record" Hogan had been hustled out of Washington and taken somewhere out West—maybe Colorado. The results from the material under analysis stayed a secret. Meanwhile the Special Prosecutor and Senate Committee resumed their focus on foreign involvement in the election.

Nick was back in New York covering crime and politics, but stayed restless. He was sure the truth of Hogan's story lay undiscovered, and convinced his boss to let him find the missing pieces. In August, Nick gave Beau his favorite toy and dropped him off with a neighbor, and then made his final trip to Utopia.

Tuesday's Return

By ten o'clock the temperature had hit ninety degrees as Nick drove the broken and bumpy two-lane blacktop to Utopia; his blue short-sleeve cotton shirt was sweat soaked. Nick never used auto air conditioners—just rolled down windows. That large boulder on the right signaled Utopia was just ahead. The lack of traffic or FBI barricades didn't surprise him, America had moved on.

Nick planned to interview everyone and return to the weeping willow tree. He drove for several miles before he realized he should have already reached his destination. The boulder he passed a while back meant he was on the right road. He turned around; after a mile he pulled to the shoulder and peered at the forest of late-summer greens mixed with sparkling red, yellow, and blue wildflowers. But, where were the broken-down buildings, the adults, the feisty kids, the dogs? Where was Utopia?

Nick paced around the area until he saw something through the heavy vegetation—the kid's soccer ball. He fished the deflated ball out and rubbed off the dirt buildup, and then tossed the ball in the trunk of his car just as a black Jeep drove by. It was the only vehicle he had seen on this road all day. The Jeep slowed and then stopped a couple hundred feet beyond Nick's car. The four occupants, dressed in light-green fatigues, stared at Nick for a minute and then drove off. Nick thought they might be hunters, and resumed his search of the area by stripping a tree branch and using it to beat back bushes and weeds.

Nick yelled at a cardinal perched in a maple tree. "Hey Little Red, what happened here? Where did these people and buildings go?"

The cardinal took off and circled around a break in the woods. Nick hurried over and recognized the dirt path that led to the weeping willow tree.

Nick glanced upward. "Little Red, we'll get to the bottom of this."

In shorts and white tennis shoes, Nick pushed back weeds and tall grass along the path, stirring up swarms of gnats as he went. After ten minutes, he stumbled toward the creek, dropped to his knees and drank, and then drowned his sweaty face in the cool water.

Nick turned to watch a rabbit munching on bright-yellow lilies. Then it hit him, the weeping willow was gone. He poked the soil where he remembered the tree stood. Soft earth told him a root ball had been ground up and removed. Nick wondered if this was more forensic study by the FBI, or the work of others. He thought of snapping a picture, but had left his cellphone and other equipment in the car.

With his hands on his hips, Nick stared at the cardinal atop a nearby rock. "Little Red, help me solve this."

The cardinal bobbed its head, and then flew downstream toward the lake.

Nick grabbed his tree-branch stick, and shouted, "Lead away."

The lake was a quarter mile. Trees and heavy underbrush snuggled up against both sides of the creek, forcing Nick to stay close to the bank. He stopped a few times to take a drink and scrape mud off his new shoes.

About half way, Nick spotted a tree stump and sat on it. Honeysuckle to his left and to his right moistened the air with a sweet aroma; a large oak tree provided shade. He watched a couple of gray squirrels on the other side of the creek chase each other over the grass, circle around a small cucumber tree, and then disappear through a stand of evergreens. A big orange butterfly came to rest on his knee; after a few minutes a delicate breeze gently swept it away. Nick thought of his son and wished he could have brought him here as a child.

Refreshed, Nick grabbed a purple wildflower and looked at the cardinal. "Little Red, a story can be hidden in a rainbow or buried under a rock, but mostly it's in front of you. If you're willing to look for it, you can find it. I'm almost there."

At one o'clock, while swinging his stick through a patch of poison ivy, Nick spotted the lake just ahead. The cardinal flew toward a white pine tree, took hold of a leafy branch, and waited as Nick approached.

The ground showed heavy foot traffic and several large wooden signs marked Private Property—No Trespassers. Hogan had said no signs had ever been posted at the lake, and everyone fished here year-round.

As Nick skirted the lake he came across an old fishing rod and wondered if those big catfish would bite this late in the day. He untangled a blue hair ribbon caught in the branches of a ruby-red hydrangea. He stared at the ribbon, and then shoved it in his back pocket.

With the cardinal watching from the pine tree, Nick dropped the fishing rod and sat down. The story had come together, and it was more than Hogan's claim or whether you believed it. It was how Hogan and others suffered because he said something the powerful and connected didn't like. Nick planned to write about the disappearance of Utopia and the brutal treatment of Hogan, about toxic arrogance from centers of political and economic power, and much more. He was going to stir things up no matter who got upset.

Around two o'clock, Nick noticed two black Jeeps approach at a high rate of speed from the far end of the lake. With the unpaved road, he figured it would be five minutes before they reached him.

Nick grabbed the fishing rod, and looked up. "Little Red, next time I'll introduce you to my son David. You'll like him; we'll all go fishing. Meanwhile, let's get out of here—I've got a story to write."

The cardinal followed Nick into the woods, and they disappeared.

Several days passed and no one at the *Journal* had heard from Nick. On Friday, Nick's boss notified local police and the FBI. A couple of weeks later the FBI informed the *Journal* that Nick's whereabouts were unknown.

Day Trip to Paradise

"This world is never as it appears to be"

Carrie's contact at the Department of Labor insisted fraud, deception, and false reports on inflation, domestic growth, and other important numbers had been released by the government bureau in charge of economic statistics. If true and word got out the financial panic would throw trillions in savings, investments, and pensions at risk around the world.

Carrie Blake was twenty-eight and a graduate of a small Midwestern college. She had spent the last five years as a business reporter for television station BTLR in St. Louis, but wanted an opportunity on a larger stage. Thin with shoulder length red hair, at nineteen she was first runner-up Miss Missouri. She lived with a white cat named Bellee in an apartment in the outer suburbs of St. Louis. Her adoptive parents died in an auto accident. There was a stepbrother Phil who lived in Los Angeles, but they hadn't talked in over two years.

On Saturday, Carrie arrived at Kirby's fast-food diner around one-thirty to meet her government source for the first time. Located thirty-five miles West of St. Louis on Hwy K, she figured it would be an ideal place to hold a quiet conversation. She had the name Steve, but didn't know what he looked like. However, he watched her on TV and said he would recognize her. She grabbed a booth near a window and waited.

At one-forty a young man with blond crew-cut hair dressed in black slacks, white shirt, and bow tie exited a blue Bronco. He glanced back toward Hwy K and around Kirby's parking lot, and then entered the restaurant.

The man strolled over, and said, "Ms. Blake, it's nice to meet you. I'm Steve McAdams."

"Hi, Steve, what you told me on the phone sounded wild, but anything is possible these days. I'll get us something to eat and we'll talk."

Carrie came back with a tray loaded with burgers and a couple of chocolate shakes. "Now tell me about you and what's going on at the Labor Department."

"I got my Ph.D. in economics last year from Washington University in New York. Since then I've worked at the U.S. Department of Labor here in St. Louis. I know numbers and the technology used to manage them, and I'm sure someone or a group of people in the government is falsifying financial information."

"How do you know that?"

"In late August, I typed in the wrong computer code at work and up popped an unfamiliar program. I realized it was designed to produce fake economic and financial data. It's real slick software, and I'm convinced it's been used to overstate some economic results, and understate other statistics reported to the public."

"You can get away with a big lie when people trust you. But why did you contact me?"

"Three weeks ago I took it to the person in charge of my department. She told me not to talk to anyone while she checked it out. Since then I haven't been able to access that program, and I feel like I'm being watched. I've got to move fast while I still can get information from the inside."

Steve leaned across the table. "I've followed your work here in town. You understand business and economics, and big shots don't intimidate you. Once you get the evidence, you'll make sure this story gets told. I haven't shared this with anyone besides you and my boss."

"My television station would never allow this story on the air until we had all the facts down to the last name and decimal."

"Ms. Blake, I'll get whatever you need."

"I want to know how things are being rigged, and be able to point a finger at those responsible. More importantly, why are they doing this—what's their motive? Creating inflation and growth rate numbers is the ultimate insider play. It allows them to make the right bets in the stock market and elsewhere. Maybe they also want to control the country through the financial system. No telling how big this might be."

Steve pointed at the window. "That's the second time that black Jeep has driven through the lot. A Jeep was behind me on Hwy 40 the last twenty miles."

"You think you've been followed?"

"Don't know, maybe I'm just getting paranoid."

A couple walked by with two noisy children in tow.

The man stopped. "Wow, Ms. Carrie Blake—I never miss when you're on."

The woman tapped Carrie's shoulder. "He loves red-heads and says you're the prettiest lady on television."

The kids ran toward the playroom and the couple gave chase.

Carrie turned to Steve. "When can you get me the information I want?"

"My access to certain programs has been restricted. I'll call you in two weeks and give you everything I've been able to pull together. I'm nervous, but committed to fighting this fraud and the people behind it."

"I won't mention this at the station until I've got enough to convince my bosses to go forward."

Carrie scanned the parking lot. "I don't see your black Jeep. I'll wait while you slip out of here."

Steve tossed the paper and plastic in the trash and left.

Carrie headed to the counter and bought a couple of warm chocolate chip cookies and a cup of coffee. She eased back into the booth and thought about the growing struggle between truth and fake—and being able to recognize the difference.

Three days later, on Tuesday morning Carrie was surprised by a call from industry superstar Beverly Janus, executive vice-president at global media giant Ganymede. Headquartered in New York, it had major offices in London, Paris, and Beijing.

Carrie squeezed her cellphone. "Ms. Janus, everyone admires your work at Ganymede. What can I do for you?"

In a soft voice, Janus said, "Carrie, we at Ganymede are aware of your fabulous research and on-air skills and feel you would be a perfect fit for an assignment that just opened. You would work here in New York as a member of the team that broadcasts news across the nation. It means national recognition and a salary at least ten times above your current pay. Would you be interested?"

Carrie glanced around her cubicle, and then said, "I'd love to work for you and Ganymede." An opportunity in the Big Apple was the call every journalist hoped to get.

"Good, I'll make the reservations for the plane and hotel. You can fly up here Friday night and be back in St. Louis by late Sunday. While you're here I'll fill you in on the job details, and when we'd like you to start. Is that OK?"

"That sounds great."

"Don't tell anyone about this offer or trip. Very few people at the network know we're adding to the team, and we don't want that information to get out. We want to make the announcement at the right time."

"I won't tell anyone. Thanks again for this opportunity."

"Then it's settled, I'll meet your flight late Friday at JFK."

Carrie's cellphone slipped out of her hand and fell to the floor. She wondered what just happened; an opportunity of a lifetime just showed up out of the blue. But it was Ganymede and New York—that's all she needed to know. She would take it.

Carrie gave her cat a long hug and kiss goodbye. "Be a good girl and don't get in any trouble. Mommy will be home Sunday night and we'll watch those nature shows you like."

Bellee grabbed her favorite toy, a pink mouse with a long fluffy tail, and ran behind the couch.

Carrie's flight landed that Friday evening around ten o'clock at JFK.

As Carrie exited the plane a husky middle-aged brunette in a tan two-button pantsuit approached. "Hello. I'm Beverly Janus, and you must be Carrie."

Carrie extended her hand. "Ms. Janus, it's nice of you to meet me."

"I'm thrilled you responded to my offer and from now on call me Beverly. I've reserved a room at the Marathon, a real nice place on Broadway. Let's grab a cab and get you settled in. It's just a fifteen-minute ride."

Carrie was eating when Beverly dropped by the hotel restaurant around nine-thirty Saturday morning.

Beverly pulled up a chair. "They serve a great breakfast, and their restaurant has been rated five-star."

Carrie held up a sugar coated donut oozing bright red jelly. "I also polished off a plate of scrambled eggs and bacon."

"My goodness, how do you stay so thin? You have to tell me your secret."

"No secret, just an active metabolism. I guess I'm lucky."

Beverly waved an empty coffee cup at the server. "Carrie, I understand you're not married. That should make your transition up here much easier."

"It's just me and my cat Bellee. She's a great companion and best friend. She's back home, probably sleeping."

"I'm married to an actor named Buzz. I pay all the bills. A cat might be a better deal."

"You can't go wrong with a cat."

Beverly leaned toward Carrie. "Are you working on any important stories that might tie you to St. Louis for a while?"

"I just started poking around questionable activities at the Labor Department, which could be a huge story."

"Wow, the Labor Department. It sounds like you got your teeth into something important there. Let's make that one of the first investigative stories you do for us."

"That's perfect."

Beverly slapped the table. "I'll pick you up at eight o'clock and we'll have dinner at a small restaurant a few blocks from here. Meanwhile, stroll around and get to know this special place. Some call it paradise."

"I will, after I finish off this donut."

Beverly laughed.

It was sunny and seventy degrees as Carrie dashed from the hotel in jeans, tennis shoes, and a bright-blue sweatshirt. First destination was Times Square where she passed a steakhouse, an oyster bar, a jazz bar, and a crowded tea salon. A bearded character in jeans and a long gray overcoat pestered her for a block trying to unload two front-row theater tickets at a thousand dollars apiece for Sunday night's performance of *The Arena*.

In front of Hardy's Liquor, an intoxicated old gentleman in green sweatpants and red-flannel shirt was yelling to passersby that he could recite any poem written by a romantic poet. Carrie requested Keats' ode *To Autumn*, and then dropped ten dollars into his plastic collection plate. The tipsy street artist stepped on a wooden crate, cleared his throat, and then delivered an eloquent recital of Keats' inspired music. When he finished, Carrie and a few others applauded. The old guy, who went by the name Lord Byron, bowed and then ran into the liquor store with his collection plate money. Carrie waited to talk to him, but when he came out of the store singing and hugging a bottle of Tequila, she decided to move on.

On 5th Avenue, young and old women exited limousines weighed down by glimmering necklaces, diamond earrings, and gem-filled broaches. Bentleys, Rolls, and Mercedes sped past.

Near the corner of 5th and East 46th Street a hundred or so people were lined up in front of a big orange circus tent. Over the tent's entrance hung a large hand painted wooden sign that proclaimed *Prestigious Shopping.*

Four men wearing ankle-length black overcoats held open the dusty tent flap as customers clutching gold-colored packages exited and others entered to the sounds of rock-n-roll music streaming from inside the tent.

Carrie approached a well-dressed couple who said they were from London. "What are they peddling inside that tent?"

The woman elbowed her male companion. "We have no idea. But, we heard Prince Charles and other famous people shop there; it's all over social media. So of course we had to come. When we get home we'll be able to tell our friends we shopped Fifth Avenue's big orange tent."

Carrie glanced at the slow moving line, and then ran across the street to a lemonade stand run by a dark-haired girl and her skinny kid brother. The small cardboard sign read fifty cents for regular and seventy-five cents for large. The little boy handed Carrie a plastic cup with extra sweetened lemonade, and in broken English reminded her to tell everyone where she bought the drink. Carrie smiled as she shoved five dollars in his torn shirt pocket, and then flagged a cab.

Carrie paid the cabbie and looked up. Embossed on the side of the building in large gold letters was 45 Rockefeller Plaza. She felt the allure, it whispered, "Step inside this special place—you'll be happy." It was all here: banking, boutiques, art, and the best damn caviar anywhere.

Carrie purchased a VIP Access ticket for thirty-four dollars, and then headed up to the Center's observation deck to take in the big view of the city.

With hundreds of others, she stood on the 70th floor and gazed at mountains of mortgaged brick, steel, glass, and concrete pushing up and out in all directions. Over on 6th Avenue, a multi-story building exhaled waves of dark-brown smoke as fire ate through its top floors. A TV helicopter hovered above while people and machines scrambled below.

With his face pushed up against the observation window, a small boy turned to his mother, and said, "Do you think that fire knows it's attacking a building here in Manhattan?"

His mother slapped him on the back of the head. "It makes no special difference just because it's Manhattan; all buildings look alike to fire. It's true; fire isn't choosy where it works or lives—or who it burns."

The boy jumped as the top floor collapsed. "Gosh—did you guys see that!"

Right across the street was St. Patrick's Cathedral and its colorful stained glass windows, bluish white Tuckahoe marble, and tan faded brick. Carrie had read it had undergone a one hundred seventy-million dollar restoration. She vowed to tour the place after she got settled in.

 On the elevator ride down, Carrie tapped a young guy on the shoulder who claimed to be a city alderman, and asked him, "Who has done more for New York, this guy Rockefeller or God?"

He shrugged his shoulders. "You definitely have to say Rockefeller."

Later, near the subway entrance on Broadway, Carrie ran into a noisy crowd enjoying a fight between a cabbie wielding a long, thick flashlight and a feisty old woman in a black leather coat brandishing a knife. No one knew or cared what the fight was about. Carrie learned the woman lived up on Park Avenue with her son, and got into fights down here about once a month.

The old lady weaved and jabbed with incredible speed and agility, keeping her foe on the defensive. With her free hand she scooped up an empty beer bottle and tossed it at the cabbie's head, and then rushed in and plunged the blade deep into his shoulder.

As the crowd cheered, a guy yelled, "Man, she nailed that dude!"

The old lady ran into a waiting limousine and tapped the driver on the shoulder. "Let's get out of here."

Carrie watched the cabbie fall to the ground, and then dialed 911. When the police arrived all they found was a lone cabbie lying in a pool of blood next to his vehicle.

On 7th Avenue a street vendor's griddle smells pulled Carrie from her odyssey. She enjoyed a foot-long juicy hotdog wrapped in cheddar cheese, a candied apple, and a frosty root beer. The vendor's name was Brian, and he put in sixteen-hour days to support a family of seven. It occurred to Carrie that a story about Brian, the guy hustling theater tickets, that drunken street poet, and maybe even that Park Avenue knife lady could supply an important perspective on Manhattan.

A little after four o'clock, Carrie cut through an alley to get back on Broadway. As she passed the rear entrance of an Italian delicatessen, a short, frail-looking woman with shoulder-length gray hair and wrinkled skin emerged from the shadows.

Draped in a black cape and holding a staff, she yelled, "Carrie, we must talk."

"Who are you, and how in the world do you know my name?"

The old woman pointed her staff at the basement door of the delicatessen. "I'm Rowna. I see the future—let's go there."

The woman appeared harmless, and reminded Carrie of one of the witches in Macbeth. Carrie held the old woman's arm as they descended four stone steps. At the bottom they squeezed through a narrow wooden door into the basement apartment.

Rowna leaned her staff against the wall and flicked the light on. "This has been my home for the last twenty-five years."

Carrie held her nose. "Whew—these odors from the deli are a bit much."

"It's just cooked salami, hot pepperoni, and spicy meatballs. You get used to it."

Carrie glanced at worn-out slacks and skirts tossed over a couple of metal folding chairs, and a wastebasket filled with candy wrappers. Stains covered a faded green couch. The concrete floor and low ceiling made Carrie feel as if she had been stuffed in a small smelly box.

Rowna unfolded a wooden card table and placed a softball sized crystal ball on its worn surface.

Carrie leaned forward. "What is that?"

"That's the ball that tells all…your past and your future."

"I know most of my past. How much will it cost to see my future?"

"Today it's free." Rowna rubbed Carrie's cheek. "I had beautiful skin like yours. I had flame red hair, and we have the same blue and fire in our eyes. Before you leave I'll show you an old photograph of me from years ago."

She struck a match to an incense burner, and then shook and chanted as she rubbed the crystal ball. Carrie assumed this gibberish was part of the act.

After a few minutes, Rowna pressed her hands over her face. "I sense terrible evil aligned against you. Leave this city now."

"Are you kidding? It's time to get a new crystal. There's a crack in that one."

"I don't joke about evil."

"What kind of evil?"

"Evil that swallows you whole."

Carrie got up. "I've heard enough."

"Settle down. I'll make us some tea, and then we'll talk."

Rowna put away the crystal, and as she walked toward the kitchen tossed Carrie a chocolate bar. "Have one of these while I heat up the water."

Carrie shoved the candy bar in her purse.

A few minutes later Rowna handed Carrie a glass of steamy black tea, and then sat next to her on the couch.

Rowna grabbed Carrie's hand. "I sense danger, and the crystal has confirmed the threat is imminent."

Carrie pulled her hand free. "What threat?"

"Evil unleashes a lot of ways. It's easy to see when it arrives all at once in an explosive rage. But when it comes slow, subtle, and smooth with a smiley face it's much more dangerous. I don't know who or what, but it's about to wrap its arms around you. And for reasons of my own, I'll always care what happens to you."

Carrie tossed twenty dollars on the table. "Thanks for the tea and the warning, but I don't run from danger."

Carrie hurried out the door into the early evening sky.

Back on Broadway, Carrie sat on a bench and wondered if the old lady had the gift or was just crazy. A mourning dove caught her attention as it circled overhead and landed in a nearby maple tree. The dove paraded back and forth on a leafless branch, and then called out "cooOOoo-woo-woo-woooo." It repeated this sorrowful call two more times and then flew across the street and coasted onto the second-floor roof of Crown's Candy.

Carrie waved at the dove, and then turned her thoughts back to that strange old fortune teller. Eventually the aroma of dark chocolate and sweet licorice smells floating from across the street became too tempting, and she headed toward the theater district.

Near the corner of 7th Avenue and West 50th Carrie gazed up as beautiful people and sugar plum fairies smiled, drank, and danced on the sides of buildings, living and loving in vibrant red, blue, and purple light shows. It was an intoxicating pitch of high-definition make-believe in the big city—a never-never land where everyone was mindlessly happy.

Carrie bummed a cigarette off a German tourist, glanced around at the light shows, and after a few drags flicked the butt in the air and headed back.

A block from the hotel, Carrie spotted folks sidestepping and jumping over a box turtle as it limped across the street.

She grabbed the creature, forced a yellow cab to slam on its brakes, and then dashed back to the sidewalk as the cabbie leaned on his horn and screamed, "You dumb-ass broad."

Carrie wagged her finger at the turtle. "Watch it, Boris. Your death won't mean anything—you're one of those that just don't count."

She rubbed gravel off its shell and then laid it in the grass. "Now get back over to Central Park where you belong. Someday I'll bring my cat Bellee and we'll visit you." The turtle snagged a noisy cricket, and then clawed its way under a baby-blue hydrangea.

Around seven-forty, Carrie arrived back at the hotel and found Beverly in the lobby.

Beverly smiled. "Let's head over to the restaurant."

"Give me a minute to wash-up and change out of these jeans."

"Casual clothes are fine—trust me."

Beverly grabbed Carrie by the arm and they joined thousands of others in a Manhattan rush to get to a theater, a restaurant, or nowhere.

While waiting at a stoplight, Beverly asked, "Carrie, how was your day trip through paradise?"

Carrie took a deep breath. "If that's paradise—it needs a lot of work."

Beverly looked over as the light changed. "We love it."

Near 8th Avenue and West 42nd Beverly pointed at a gated street of Victorian-style homes. "We turn down there and it's on the left. I've got reservations for eight o'clock. They cater to a very exclusive clientele here in New York and from around the world. You won't see a sign or doorman out front. No valet parking. Everyone walks or gets dropped off—the street is closed to through traffic."

"If it's that exclusive, how did I qualify?"

"I made the arrangements and told them how important you are. They didn't argue."

Leaves rattled over the stone pavement, pushed by a warm autumn breeze. Gas lamp posts lined the sidewalk along with black oak trees. The crack of a tree branch caused Carrie to look up as a gray squirrel leapt from one limb to another.

Beverly stopped at 1307—a large two-story brick structure surrounded by a cast iron fence. She unlocked its heavy gate, and Carrie followed her over a gravel path to a big wooden porch where a green light glowed above the door.

Carrie inhaled the sugary scent of late blooming roses as she gazed into the yard. "Nature's perfume is so sweet—so delicious, and the lawn is gorgeous. Who lives here?"

Beverly pressed the doorbell. "It's where important people meet."

A tall blond named Yvette welcomed them into a two-story foyer carpeted with a dark-blue rug. Against the wall to the left was a large grandfather clock, and straight ahead a massive oak staircase led to the second floor. Two bearded men in jeans and black turtleneck sweaters stood at the top of the stairs. Hand guns protruded from their waistbands.

Yvette escorted them through a narrow hallway to a room with a scuffed hardwood floor and light gray plaster walls. A floor-to-ceiling brick fireplace anchored the front of the room. Three large crystal chandeliers hung from the twelve-foot ceiling. Five wooden tables sat about fifteen-feet apart. Each table could accommodate six.

After seating them, Yvette said, "Your party is the first to arrive. What would you like to drink?"

Beverly said, "We'd like a bottle of merlot."

Carrie noticed letters sown into the white tablecloths. "What does this BWB stand for?"

"BWB is an acronym for a nonprofit foundation devoted to building a more perfect world."

"I wonder which slippery path they're using this time—from the right or the left."

Beverly stared at Carrie, and then lit a cigarette. "This place seats thirty and opens at eight o'clock. It has the best wine cellar in New York. There's no walk-in trade. You need a reservation, and must have a key to that gate. It's got a great kitchen and world-class chef. I ordered us each a well-done porterhouse steak. I got you a side of French fries, and I went with green beans."

Carrie thought a moment. "What's up on the second floor that you need armed guards?"

"There are bedrooms up there for VIPs that want their presence secret while in town. I don't even know who stays there. The guns are mostly for show. I don't think they've had to shoot anyone for a while."

"I hope they choose their targets carefully."

After a few minutes, four men in blue pin-stripe suits walked through the door and sat at the table to Carrie's immediate left.

Beverly whispered, "Those are investment bankers. Two live in London and the others work out of Zurich. That blond-headed guy is under thirty and worth at least five billion. I've been to his chateau in the Swiss Alps—fabulous."

Over the next ten minutes the other tables filled. There was a middle-aged couple—he in a white tuxedo and she in a cream-colored dress.

Next to arrive, a group of Asians, three men and two women in green sweaters with the letters BWB on the back. All looked in their mid-thirties. Then an old man in gray slacks and red sweater carrying a tan Cairn terrier sat in the corner and ordered a scotch.

The sizzling twelve-ounce steaks smothered in sautéed onions and mushrooms arrived along with a bottle of wine.

Beverly raised her glass. "Carrie, we'll drink to that better world. It's time we give the people one."

"Is it yours to give? By the way, what do they call this place?"

Beverly finished her wine. "No name just numbers—1307. A couple hundred New Yorkers, another hundred from Washington, and a few thousand from around the world have keys that unlock that front gate. You get a key and the telephone number by invite."

The meaty scent of fresh-cooked steak and quiet conversation settled in and gave the place the feel of a small-town diner. Carrie glanced around and wondered what the powerful would decide tonight. Maybe they would put someone in charge of a company or country? Or would they decide war or peace somewhere. Perhaps they were figuring who gets more and who stays hungry? It bothered her that much power lay in the shadows controlled by so few.

Around nine-thirty, after everyone had finished dinner, the lights dimmed and a fat gentleman in a black cape, tuxedo, top hat, with a cane in one hand and a jug in the other entered the room. His gray hair drooped over his shoulders. A thick white beard smothered his face. Two assistants dragged in a large trunk.

The man set the jug down, and then swept the air with his cane. "I'm the Great Yorick, jester and illusionist."

Carrie applauded. "That guy reminds me of a history professor I had back in the day—the same belly and beard. Is Yorick clever?"

Beverly replied, "He will mesmerize you."

Yorick took a long drink from the jug, and then lifted a jewelry box from the trunk. He held up a necklace studded with diamonds and brilliant emeralds, and then tossed it in the air where it seemed to disappear. Yorick shook his head in bewilderment, and then walked over to Carrie and asked if he could look in her purse. She obliged, and out he pulled the necklace.

Carrie clapped while everyone else gently tapped their table.

Beverly pointed at the necklace. "Carrie, you could retire and live a long comfortable life on what that's worth."

Yorick took a drink, and continued a performance that included cards, rabbits, and birds. He even told a few jokes.

Beverly asked the server for a special merlot.

The bottle arrived as Carrie focused on Yorick's performance.

Carrie smelled the bouquet and took a sip. "This is so delicate and sweet."

Yorick called for a volunteer to close the performance. The old man with the terrier raised his hand. Yorick retrieved a large red silk cloth from the trunk. His two assistants stretched the cloth in front of the man, hiding him and the terrier from view. Yorick waved his cane and chanted a Latin verse, and then his assistants dropped the silk cloth to the floor. The man and his dog had disappeared.

Carrie stumbled over and examined the empty table and chair. She stomped for a trap door; a couple of boards squeaked, but no sign of man or dog.

Feeling the wine, Carrie shoved her finger into Yorick's chest. "Illusionist, what did you do with them."

Yorick smiled. "This world is never as it appears to be."

Carrie pushed the table. "Illusionists depend on fooling people. But, we're not all fools."

Beverly walked Carrie back to their table while Yorick bowed to an ovation.

In a slurred voice, Carrie said, "He's clever, but before I leave I'll figure it out." As the place emptied she fell unconscious.

Carrie woke a little after twelve o'clock Sunday morning. Her purse and cellphone had been taken, and she was propped in a chair while a makeup artist buffed on lipstick and a beautician pulled her shoulder-length red hair into a ponytail.

The makeup artist held a mirror to Carrie's face. "That slight boost of pink adds to the allure—beautiful. You should be in the movies."

Still groggy, Carrie glanced around the room. "Where am I? What the hell is this?"

The makeup artist shrugged. "Ms. Beverly told us to get you ready. I don't know any more than that."

Beverly appeared with two guys dressed in security outfits that looked like armored car drivers. "We want you to look your best for the production."

Carrie grabbed Beverly by the arm. "What's going on?"

She shoved Carrie back into the chair. "You stumbled onto information about one of our financial programs we won't let you share with the public."

Beverly began to walk away. "By the way, you're at the Olympian theater on 42nd Street. The greatest Broadway stars of the last fifty-years have performed on this stage. I'll have someone get you a cup of coffee to help clear your head. You're smart, you can figure this out."

Carrie refused the coffee and thought about the crystal ball reader. Was Rowna right? Carrie stared at the security guards who resembled heavyweight wrestlers, and figured she would have to play this hand out.

The clock on the wall showed twelve-thirty. There was the sound of furniture dragged over wooden floors, chairs dropped in place, and Beverly's voice ordering people and placement of objects.

Beverly appeared at the dressing-room door in a blond wig with long pigtails and a very tight navy-blue fairy godmother outfit. "Carrie, it's time to go. You'll be seated on stage, but any sounds or disruptions and we'll strap you in and tape your mouth shut. Do you understand?"

Led by Beverly and flanked by two security guards they walked a short distance and seated Carrie in a tan leather swivel chair on the right side of the stage facing the audience. On the other side a young woman with red hair and young man dressed like her contact at the Labor Department sat across from each other at a wooden table. Carrie now understood her investigation into financial misconduct at the government was the root of all of this.

The security men stood off stage while Beverly walked in front of the curtain.

Beverly faced the audience and bowed, and then swung her fairy godmother wand in the air. "Thanks for coming on such short notice. Tonight's production is titled *The Tragedy of Carrie Blake.*

Our cast includes Kelly O'Rourke as ace reporter Carrie Blake, and Danny Kirk in the role of the snoopy Labor Department analyst named Steve McAdams. The real Carrie Blake is seated on stage to your right. Our production opens at a fast-food restaurant in the outer suburbs of St. Louis, where the principles met and plotted against our interests."

As the curtain rose, Beverly said, "Let's give our performers a nice welcome."

Carrie leaned forward; bunched in the first two rows of the otherwise empty theater were twenty hand-clapping, foot-stomping men and women dressed in clown outfits.

Over the next fifteen minutes the actors repeated word-for-word Carrie's conversation with her informant.

During the twenty-minute break, cool jazz beamed over the speakers as Carrie and the security people stared at each other. The table and chairs had been carried off and replaced by a speaker podium at center stage.

Beverly approached, and pointed the wand. "Carrie, curtain rises in two minutes. Very important people have arrived and I don't want any trouble from you."

"Get screwed."

The curtain rose and three new arrivals stood in a balcony box about forty feet to Carrie's left. Looking down with their smiley faces, they included two U.S. Supreme Court Justices and the president of Ganymede. Carrie recognized them and waved, but got no response.

Beverly saluted the folks in the balcony, and then faced the clowns. "You heard the evidence. That red-head seated over there along with an analyst at the Labor Department planned to expose and unravel one of our most important programs. We control financial information reported by government. If we want to show strong growth and low inflation—we do it. We show high inflation if it serves our purpose.

We've managed the financial system for quite a while, and don't intend to let anyone interfere with that right."

The clowns jumped up and clapped, blew horns, and whistled.

Beverly signaled for quiet. "Mr. Steven McAdams was a smart boy and had most of this figured out, but he's no longer a threat. Then there's Carrie Blake. That pretty lady over there is smart, independent, and thinks too much. Challenges like that are dealt with in a swift fashion."

Beverly handed Carrie a piece of paper. "Sign this."

Carrie read the typed statement. "Why should I?"

"We can forge your signature, but prefer your cooperation."

Carrie glanced at the security people, and then stood and faced the folks in the balcony. "I'll sign under two conditions. First, guarantee that someone takes care of my cat Bellee. She's expecting me home later today. Also, I want ten minutes to say something to those clowns."

The folks in the balcony huddled for a moment, and then the president of Ganymede signaled thumbs up.

 Carrie signed, tossed the pen in the air, and then faced the clowns. "They've given me ten minutes, so let's make the most of it.

"I confess I had begun to look into shenanigans at the Labor Department. I confess to being a threat to that program and the people behind it.

"I confess I'm committed to the truth and exposing fake, fraud, and half-truths.

"I confess to being offended by the moral smugness behind tonight's production.

"I confess to being tempted by this garden of glitter, wealth, and power. You get to travel first-class, relax in a multi-million dollar condo, know so-called celebrities, eat caviar with a shovel, and live without guilt. But don't be fooled by that shiny stuff; it rubs off and you find it's really a shallow place manned by a shallow cast of characters."

Carrie pointed. "Some of you have red hair; others have green, blue, and a few even have orange. There's white, black, and light gray makeup, and it's about even between long and short noses. Those cosmetic differences mean nothing. You're all the same, just a bunch of clowns. You laugh together, boo in unison, celebrate and frown at the same time. I noticed a few of you looked around to see how others responded before doing anything that might embarrass you. No one wants to be out of pitch."

Carrie looked at Beverly, and then glanced at the balcony. "The powerful need clowns, fools, and jesters for their dark soulless nights. Clowns are compliant; clowns keep each other in check, and clowns don't think—they just do the dirty work.

"Look at them up there in that box. They tell you who to admire and who to hate, and what you're supposed to believe. We've felt that ill wind before…*haven't we?*

"Discover your voice and with it comes your spirit. Strip off those damn costumes—and then the folks in the balcony will fear you."

Beverly stepped forward. "That's enough, Carrie."

Carrie turned to Beverly. "I decided at the restaurant I didn't want any part of this place."

Carrie then yelled to the clowns. "This story needs a hero, and truth is a great cause for heroes. Truth will turn their so-called paradise upside down."

The security people laughed while a clown with orange hair seemed to be nodding in agreement.

Sunday morning around eleven-forty news reports mentioned the discovery of a young woman's body at the downtown Marathon Hotel. First stories hinted she had been assaulted and stabbed to death in her hotel room. The NYPD scheduled a news conference for that afternoon.

At one-thirty, detective Dave Holly addressed a small crowd of reporters in the lobby of the Marathon. "They called us right after the cleaning crew discovered the body around ten-thirty this morning. Forensics has spent a couple of hours inside the hotel room of this unfortunate young woman. Clutched in her hand was a typed suicide note signed by her. There are no indications of trauma on the body, and preliminary examination by the medical team suggests some kind of drug overdose."

A reporter asked, "Was she someone famous or important?"

Detective Holly shrugged his shoulders. "Her driver's license says she's Carrie Blake from St. Louis. I never heard of her, but I guess she's important to someone."

"What's she doing in New York?"

"The suicide note says she came here to die. If that's the case, this will be the third suicide at this hotel in the last four months. Anyway, she worked for a small television station in St. Louis, and was upset about a lack of progress in her career."

A reporter was overheard saying, "It doesn't take much these days to send people over the edge."

The body, covered in a white sheet, was wheeled past in a gurney. A gray-haired woman wearing a black cape and dragging a staff followed the gurney out the door.

The Special Prosecutors

"We don't want illegals on campus. We'll fight for their rights elsewhere."

A family of deplorables had moved in across the street and Jerry knew something had to be done to protect his gated world.

Jerry Garga was seventeen and lived with his parents and younger brother Fudgie—real name Harry—in a six thousand square-foot white-brick ranch home. Leafy palm trees and lush green lawns covered the neighborhood, while beds of red roses and soft-blue lilacs sweetened its breezy Malibu air. Carbon Beach was less than a mile away.

Tall, tanned, with shoulder-length brown hair, Jerry was heading into his senior year at Ocean Side high school. He drove a high-powered bright-orange convertible, had visited Paris, and vacationed on the Greek islands. Studio executives, movie and rock stars were his neighbors.

Jerry felt something was wrong the day that family arrived in early July. First, it was the Georgia plates on their cars, then the dad had a scruffy brown beard, and wore a red plaid shirt and cowboy hat and boots. He looked like a clod from the backwoods.

As Jerry watched the furniture get unloaded, Fudgie ran up, and said, "Those kids talk with weird accents. And look at that pickup truck the guy got out of."

Jerry shook his head. "God, I'll bet they like country music and own guns."

Jerry learned the family's name was Miller and the dad was a senior executive with Allied-Sun, a corporation with a large chemical and carbon footprint in Asia. The kids had been enrolled at a private middle school. The mom remained a mystery, but Jerry had snapped her photo and planned to circulate it on social media sites to see if anyone might recognize her.

Founded in 1925, Ocean Side was a private high school always ranked near the top based on statewide test scores. California's current governor, two U.S. Supreme Court Justices, and the president of a major media conglomerate were Ocean Side graduates. Its two-hundred acres included two Olympic size swimming pools, planetarium, a just-finished three-thousand seat theater, and expanded dorms to accommodate seventy-five out-of-state students. Annual tuition was sixty thousand.

Classes at Ocean Side began Monday, August 16th. Jerry needed to pass Ms. Brown's course in Social Activism for graduation. They discussed his project idea, and she gave her quick approval. Now he needed a team to move things along.

On Friday, that first week of school, Jerry met with fellow seniors Ashley, Jessica, Mike, and Carolyn around three-thirty in a classroom near the cafeteria.

After they pulled their desks in a circle, Jerry said, "Ms. Brown gave her approval for this project, so we'll get course credit when it's done." He looked at his team, and grinned. "A family of deplorables moved across the street from me, and we have until the end of the semester, about four months, to get them out of there to save the neighborhood."

Ashley clapped. "Damn, what a fun project."

Carolyn shook her head. "Jerry, what the hell is a deplorable?"

"Where've you been? They're barbarians. Uneducated, uncouth, and when they have college degrees it's from some place you never heard of. Even rich ones like their guns and bible—the kind of people you don't want living across the street. They'll tear your neighborhood down if you allow them in. I'm calling this project *Deplorables at the Gate*."

Mike laughed as he wadded a piece of paper and tossed it at the waste can.

Carolyn stared at the others. "So we're going to bully people—including kids?"

Jessica took a drink from her diet soda, and then grabbed Carolyn by the arm. "Calm down, Ms. Brown has approved this project. Plus, we need this credit to graduate."

Carolyn scooted her desk back, and got up. "I'll create something positive with my senior project. This sounds like arrogant nonsense aimed at people that might think and look a little different than you. It stinks Ms. Brown approved this junk. I'll find another team to work with."

Carolyn turned as she reached the door. "How many people will you guys hurt saving the neighborhood?" She slammed the door.

Jerry strolled to the blackboard. "We don't need that red-headed jerk. Jessica, dig up everything you can about Mrs. Kathy Miller. I've got a couple of pictures I'll send you. She's in her mid-thirties, blond and blue-eyed, with a great figure. We need to get some juicy stuff; I'll bet she's played around. They're from Georgia, but go wherever it takes you."

"I'll get on that."

"Ashley, find stuff on the kids Chet and Rebecca. They attend the middle school my brother is at. Get a copy of their transcripts submitted to the school district. Maybe there's a history of crappy grades, or they flunked somewhere along the line. It would be even better if they ever got suspended."

Ashley began writing in her notebook. "I know where your brother goes to school. My old babysitter works at the administrative offices over there, and she would have access. But, it would cost us. She won't do it without pay."

"Here's the good news. I told my dad about this project and he gave me five thousand dollars to cover any expenses. Offer whatever it takes to get those transcripts."

"I know she'll sell, I'll get us the best price I can."

"If we need more money I can get it."

Around four-fifty a janitor looked in. "We need to clean this room."

Jerry waved. "Give us five minutes, and we'll be out of here." He erased the board, and said, "Mike, you and me will get the dad, Ben

Miller. We'll also research his employer Allied-Sun. Maybe we can bring some heat on the Millers through his workplace. When we're done that family will run, not walk, out of my neighborhood. Next time we'll meet over at the church."

A rattle of drums and blare of trumpets and trombones announced the pep rally.

Jessica said, "Jerry, let's head to the football field. My brother is on the team, I think he's a receiver or something. I'm sure the Yellow Jackets will be better this year. Go, gold!"

"Great idea. After that we'll go to my house for beer and pizza. I'll pay for it with some of the project's money. We'll call it an entertainment expense, just like a real business."

Everyone laughed.

Ocean Side's social conscious was always on display. Classroom walkouts and rallies against injustice averaged two a month. A list of preferred boycotts, updated weekly, got posted at the entrance of all school buildings. Activists were perpetually shaking a fist or wagging a righteous finger somewhere on campus. The school's *We Care More* foundation funded social justice all over the world.

The last week in September, Jerry's team met Friday night at the old church. Located at the center of campus, it was the first structure built back in the Twenties. The large white cross atop its golden dome reached one hundred feet; it was visible twenty miles in all directions. The faded brick façade, twenty-foot oak entry doors, blue-gray marble floors, and stained-glass windows remained an important legacy to some, but an eyesore and wasted space to most. It could seat three hundred in its thirty rows of wooden pews. The church hadn't had a regular chaplain for twenty-five years, but remained open day and night for anyone to stop by.

Jerry lit a dozen candles, and then faced his team sitting in a pew a few feet away. "We'll work by candlelight."

Ashley whispered, "This place is spooky."

Jerry turned the lights out, and sat down. "It's supposed to be spooky; it's a church. Now what about those kids Chet and Rebecca? And, we don't need to whisper."

Ashley reached into her purse and handed Jerry a stack of papers. "These transcripts cost five hundred bucks. Great grades and no problem with authorities—they seem like a couple of smart angels."

"We'll just find another way to go after them. My brother Fudgie can help. He goes to school there. He's already got rumors started about them, and their accents make them stand out. What we need is a negative incident at the school that traces back to them. I'll get with my brother and figure that out."

Jerry held up a photo. "Jessica, what has this hot-looking lady been up to?"

"She grew up in Georgia, and modeled for some department stores in the Atlanta area. Then she married that guy Miller at twenty-two. Ten years ago she had a couple of speeding tickets, and got involved in a minor accident. She creased a car door in a church lot. She's helped with a couple of charities, and raised those two kids. That's all I got so far."

"What about brothers, sisters, parents, or crazy uncles? And find out if those charities are clean, a lot of them are phonies these days. Maybe we can discover or generate a scandal by extension. Also, post Kathy Miller's picture on as many sites as possible down in Georgia, and offer five hundred dollars for any negative information on that babe. We'll use the two wildest stories. For that kind of money there will be a lot of takers."

Jerry stretched out in the pew. "I paid a couple of neighbor kids a few hundred bucks to tail Daddy Miller around town the last couple of weeks. They said he visits a shooting range, so he owns and likes to use guns. He also stopped at a country western bar a couple of times—without his wife. Mike's researched Miller's company Allied-Sun and found it dumps pollution in the ground and air over in Asia. Not a lot, but we can build a few bonfires from that."

Ashley pointed toward the altar. "Look." There was a flapping sound from a figure hovering over the pulpit, and then it disappeared. She slapped Jerry on the shoulder. "What the hell is that?"

"Calm down, that's no damn spook. It's a mourning dove that's been hanging out at the church for thirty years."

Mike shook his head. "Doves live maybe five years."

Jerry lit a couple more candles. "My dad graduated here back in the Eighties, and he told me the story behind the dove. It began when a workman discovered a student's body sprawled on the altar with a rope wrapped around the neck and his face all bruised up. The guy came from a wealthy family out of Japan. A mourning dove showed up soon after and has been at the church ever since. I don't know if it's the same dove, or a series of doves. My dad said at the time there were rumors that the chaplain did the killing. But, that's a mystery that never got solved."

Jessica leaned forward. "Jerry, are you saying this place is haunted by that dead guy's spirit trapped in a dove?"

"Don't be stupid, no one believes in holy spirits or saints anymore. But it's a neat old-time story."

Mike glanced through torn yellowed pages in a prayer book. "Back in the Fifties I'll bet these pews were packed Sundays with students and faculty praying, singing, and hanging on the words of a righteous minister pointing the path to salvation. It must have been quite a show. No one sings or weeps here anymore. All that's left is dust, old prayer books, that big brown organ over there, and a crazy dove." He tore a page out of the prayer book and shoved it in his pocket.

Jessica waved a prayer book above her head and laughed. "They must have had a lot more sinners back then—halleluiah."

The dove whizzed past Jerry's head, landed on a window ledge, and began to coo and pace back and forth.

Jerry grabbed an unlit candle and flung it at the dove. It shattered against the wall a few feet below the dove. The dove stared at the chunks of broken wax and then flapped its wings.

Jerry said, "Let's get out of here. We'll meet back here in about six weeks; by then we'll have those deplorables shaking in their grungy boots."

In October, Ocean Side's faculty voted to impeach the president again, students discovered three new injustices to demonstrate against, and the football team lost all its games.

Jerry told his brother to go after Chet and Rebecca at the middle school. First, Fudgie drew a bright red swastika in the boy's bathroom, and then some of his friends spread the story around school that Chet had done it. Chet got suspended on the seventeenth after school security found a bright red magic marker with alt-right paraphernalia in his locker.

After Chet's suspension, Jerry called his dad's friend at KPMH, an LA TV station, and they rushed a crew to the middle school and interviewed parents and students—including Fudgie, about the racially charged incident. Chased by cameras, the school principal ran to her car and drove off. The story headlined KPMH's news at five. The next day Rebecca punched a classmate that called her brother a racist, and also got suspended.

On Halloween, around eleven-thirty Fudgie set off a case of fireworks in the Miller's front yard, and then laughed from his bedroom window as the police and fire department arrived.

The second week of November, Jerry got an after-school job in the news department at an LA TV station owned by media giant Ganymede. He helped around the office, ran errands, and even got to ride along with reporters on stories. Also, his Ivy League school of choice accepted his application for the next fall—he intended to major in journalism. His dad had connections at both places. He celebrated by getting drunk with friends at the beach.

Saturday night, five days before Thanksgiving, Mike, Ashley, and Jessica were waiting at the church.

Ashley checked her cellphone. "It's ten after twelve, where the hell is Jerry? There are better things to do than hanging out in this musty old place."

Mike scanned the altar and then looked up. "I don't see the dove. If Jerry doesn't show in five minutes, I'll send him a text."

Just then the door swung open and Jerry, in tennis shoes, jeans, and bright-blue sweatshirt, ran down the center aisle clutching a can of beer.

Jerry took a drink, and then tossed the empty can toward the altar. "I got a ticket on the way over. They said I did thirty-five miles over the speed limit. I'm glad the bastards didn't check the trunk of my car. I've a case of beer stashed there for later tonight."

Jerry lit a few candles and an incense stick, flicked the lights out, and then stood at the lectern. "Let's move this along. The Miller kids got suspended in October, they might even expel Chet. We can thank Fudgie and some of his friends for getting that done. The school is freaking out about all the bad publicity on television, and now all over social media. Oh yeah, Halloween night my crazy brother caught the Miller's lilac shrubs on fire. You should have seen old Ben Miller out there with a hose trying to put it out. What fun.

"Jessica, did you get any hot stories on Mrs. Miller?"

"I posted her name and picture and asked for something wild about the lady. Offer five-hundred bucks and folks crawl out from under rocks. A guy sent a photo of a naked woman straddling a horse. He insists it's our Mrs. Miller, but I think it's photo-shopped with her head onto the body of another woman. He did a good job, and it might fool a lot of people. I also got a long response from the mother of a lifer named Clyde at the Georgia state prison at Reidsville. She claims her son dated Kathy Miller, and they used to party, do drugs, and rob places together. I doubt it, but I decided to go with the story."

Jerry tapped the lectern. "Send out hard copies of that horse picture to the principal in charge of her kids' middle-school, and another to her husband. Then get that story about Clyde with a picture of Mrs. Miller out on social media sites, and include the Millers' address. That should raise the heat in that household."

"I'll post that crap tomorrow. I'm amazed what fake news can accomplish."

"Jessica, there's no such thing as fake news. Whether it's true or not doesn't have anything to do with news. It's real once it's out there creating images, driving attitudes, and getting things done. Politicians use made-up stories so people feel good about them and bad about others—and it works. Businessmen, governments, ministers, activists—they all manipulate and peddle their own narratives. That's all we're doing."

Jessica shrugged. "I guess you're right."

"You bet I'm right. Now let's hear from Mike."

"Guys, this is cool. Last Tuesday, I planted a story on social media about Allied-Sun—Miller's employer. According to the story, twenty-five years ago Allied-Sun had a chemical spill from a plant that wiped out a village in rural Northern China. To hush the thing up, Allied-Sun delivered a secret fifty-million dollar payment to the Chinese Government. I set the death toll at twelve-hundred, and had the village bulldozed over to make it impossible to locate. And here's the topper, I made Ben Miller the young plant manager. I also suggest he's blackmailed his way up the corporate ladder because he's one of the few that knows about this story."

Ashley shook her head. "I saw your story, but Allied-Sun, Miller, and the Chinese will just deny all this, and without proof that will kill it."

"You're wrong, because stories with conspiracy and cover-up don't run on proof. People want to believe it and lack of proof is part of the cover-up. Deniability doesn't count—that's gold. I'm sure Miller and his bosses are scrambling to find a way to respond. Allied-Sun's stock dropped over twenty points the last few days. Investors know perception is reality—that's the only truth that matters."

Jerry slapped the lectern. "Great job Mike, maybe they'll get rid of Miller to cut their losses. We got things moving in the right direction, and have about thirty days to reach our goal of getting them out of there. I've updated Ms. Brown, and she's confident we'll get the job done. She called the principal at the middle-school to demand a plan of action to weed out student bigotry. She promised us extra credit if a plan goes into effect. Now that's a hands-on educator.

"I've got another piece of good news, but the dove won't like it. My dad is on the board here, and he tells me the thick walls of this church will come tumbling down next June and be replaced with metal benches, modern art, and roses. It will be a common ground where people can relax and reflect. That's a better use of the space."

Ashley made the sign of the cross. "Amen, I get the creeps every time we come to this dreary place."

Mike got up, and said, "Jerry, have they thought about using the church as a sanctuary, or maybe convert it into a homeless shelter?"

"Are you fucking crazy? We don't want bums and illegals on our campus. We can fight for their rights elsewhere."

As they left, Jessica turned to Jerry. "I ran into Carolyn in the cafeteria the other day, and she said her senior project has raised over twenty-five thousand dollars for an animal rescue facility in East LA."

Jerry raised his middle finger. "Screw Carolyn."

Jerry reached the parking lot and noticed a dove circle a light post and then head toward his car. As he opened the door, the bird splattered shit all over his car's hood and driver side windshield, and then flew toward the church.

The first week of December, three students circulated a petition protesting the demolition of the church, not on religious but architectural grounds as an historic building. Two fellow students and one faculty member signed.

Christmas hadn't been recognized at Ocean Side for fifteen years; decorations on campus were prohibited as offensive exhibits of Western culture. Security removed and burnt three Merry Christmas posters, and investigated a rumor that a Christmas wreath had been smuggled into one of the dorm rooms. Students had to report anything suspicious.

For the second year in a row the football team failed to win a game.

Jerry's gated community was quiet in December; most homeowners holidayed at a Riviera beach or Alpine slope. Jerry's parents liked Asia this year; they left the boys on the tenth, would celebrate the New Year in Shanghai, and be back a few days later.

On the fifteenth of December, around five in the afternoon a large moving van backed into the Miller's driveway and four men began to load household furniture on the truck.

Jerry called Fudgie, and pointed across the street. "I'll get my team; use your phone to record this."

By seven o'clock, Ashley, Jessica, and Mike gathered on Jerry's front lawn. Relaxing in lawn chairs with an ice chest loaded with beer, they cheered when a bedroom set got carried to the truck.

Jerry handed Fudgie a beer. "Make sure you catch the van as it pulls out."

A little after nine o'clock the van departed. Around nine-thirty Mrs. Miller and her daughter Rebecca got in the gray sedan, and Mr. Miller and Chet jumped in the white pickup.

As they pulled out of the driveway, Jerry shouted, "Fuck you and that damn pickup."

Jessica said, "Are we done?"

Jerry stared at the empty home. "We'll take a victory lap over there—then we're done. You guys grab another beer while I get a couple of flashlights."

A few minutes later they forced open a door at the rear of the abandoned home. Mike used the bathroom in the master suite, while the others ventured around. They found a ten-foot artificial Christmas tree in the family room. Ashley plugged it in and the dark room sparkled blue and green as the colored lights bounced and reflected off frosty metallic ornaments. Layers of bright red and silver garland hugged the tree. On top a shiny white star blinked on and off while it played *Away in a Manger* and *Silent Night*.

Ashley squeezed the soft garland. "This is beautiful. Maybe I can talk my parents into putting up one of these things. There's still time."

Jerry grabbed a blue ornament embossed with small golden angels and handed it to his brother. "Fudgie, here's a souvenir. You did as much as anyone to get our win. Let's all grab an ornament. We'll leave the tree lights on."

Jerry sent Ms. Brown a text message with a picture of the tree.

Five minutes later, Jerry commented on Ms. Brown's response. "She loves what we've accomplished, we're getting an A. I'll steal a couple bottles of my dad's wine, and then we celebrate at the beach."

As they left, Fudgie slapped his brother on the back. "Do I get credit for helping run these deplorables out of here?"

"You'll have to settle for an ornament this time. Don't worry, next year you'll be at Ocean Side, and they'll find plenty of these opportunities for you."

A Farewell to Nick

"Hate shows you care."

Nick Cyrus, long-time reporter for the *Journal*, was missing. His last known whereabouts was an August assignment in rural Tennessee. In September, Nick's thirty-five year-old-son David was located in Chicago and told of his father's disappearance by Jake Peters, Nick's boss at the *Journal*.

At six-foot, a little overweight with wavy shoulder-length blond hair, David Cyrus resembled a younger version of his dad. He tended bar at Pat's Saloon located on the corner of Rush Street and American Avenue. His weekends were spent traveling the Chicagoland area performing Shakespeare with a six-member acting troupe known as The Players. David earned enough to pay for a one-bedroom apartment in a rundown neighborhood on Chicago's north side.

David, an only child, hadn't talked to his dad for over ten years, from about the time his mother had died. Their estranged relationship had drifted into indifference.

In early October, David took a week off from his job, told his friends to find a temporary replacement in the acting troupe, packed a suitcase, and Sunday morning got on I-80 in his faded green Jeep. He had a one o'clock appointment the next day with Jake Peters in New York.

David arrived in New York around twelve-thirty Monday afternoon, and drove to 40 Wall Street. On the 57th floor he entered the home of the *Journal* through a pair of thick glass doors. Fifty minutes later, a short, fat man wearing a gray pin-striped suit introduced himself as

Jake Peters, editor of the *Journal*. David's jeans, tennis shoes, and blue sweatshirt were out of place in this suit-and-tie world.

On the way to Peters' corner office, David passed rows of noisy orange cubicles and the aroma of fresh-brewed coffee.

David took a seat in the sprawling office while Peters strolled to his wall of windows and pointed toward the financial district. "That's where the sun rises and they print the gold that pays for all this."

Peters eased into his big black leather chair, threw his feet up on his desk, and grinned. "This town is different—we're different."

"You said my dad was chasing a wild story, and then disappeared."

"That's right. Some nut made a crazy claim about the presidential election that caught fire for fifteen-minutes and then died out. But Nick wouldn't let it go. It was tabloid stuff, but I allowed your dad to talk me into one final trip to that place in Tennessee just to get it out of his system."

"That sounds like my dad. Once he gets a hold of a story he follows it to its conclusion. I remember his instincts as a journalist. Maybe he found something?"

"Nah, there was nothing down there. It was about a guy who said he talked to God, or God talked to him—I forget. No reason to disappear over that."

"But he's disappeared. Why?"

"After he failed to check in with me, I called the state police and the FBI. Both said there was no sign of him. I told you over the phone they found his rental car parked outside a strip club in Memphis. The FBI reported two-hundred dollars on his credit cards was used inside that club."

"And I told you my dad never visited strip clubs."

"David, too much booze can make anyone lose control. Your old-man was quite the drinker at one time. He put the bottle away a couple of years ago, but maybe he found an excuse to fall off the wagon and it led somewhere else. Anyway, that's what it looked like to the FBI."

"Well, what happened after that?"

"The trail ended in Memphis. All I can say is Nick was different."

"You said 'was' in referring to my dad. Do you think he's dead?"

"Hell, I don't know if he's dead. But, he doesn't work here anymore. We needed someone to cover his beat, so he's been replaced."

David leaned across the desk. "Shit. After ten years—just like that."

Peters tossed David a set of keys. "We found these when we cleaned out your dad's desk. I think one is for his brownstone, and the other looks like a car key. We've got a box with his things. His address in the Village is written on the side of the box."

Peters set his horn-rimmed glasses on his desk, escorted David outside his office, and signaled his secretary. "Cathy, get that stuff of Nick's and give it to this gentleman." Peters then headed back in his office and closed the door.

A few minutes later Cathy handed David a cardboard box. "Here you go."

She pointed at the cubicles. "I can show you where your dad sat and worked."

"Nah, one cubicle is the same as another."

David glanced at the box. On top was a framed picture of him at seven years, dressed in suit and tie. At the bottom of the photograph his dad had written, "David's First Holy Communion."

It was a twenty-five minute drive from the *Journal*'s office to Nick's home in the Village. David parked, grabbed the box and walked toward his dad's brownstone.

As David unlocked the front door, a skinny woman with shoulder-length gray hair ran up. "I guess you're David. I'm Irene from next door."

"Yep, I'm David. You must know my dad."

"I've liked him since he moved in over ten years ago. But Nick's been gone for months, and I still have his cat Beau. I've left messages on his cellphone. Do you know when he'll be back?"

"Come in and I'll bring you up to date."

David set the box on the floor while Irene opened a kitchen cabinet and took out a couple of shot glasses and a bottle of scotch.

She filled the glasses. "Your dad and I used to polish off one of these bottles every now and then. But, he quit cold. I haven't seen him drink in a couple of years. I guess he kept this around just in case. Here you go."

They downed the shots, Irene poured another, and then they sat on a beige cloth-covered couch.

David set his ball cap on the coffee table. "Here's the scoop. Dad disappeared down in Tennessee while working on a story. No one has seen or heard from him since August."

"What did the folks at the *Journal* say?"

"They shoved his stuff in that box and moved on. That's what ten years buys in this town."

"Those fucking bastards! Your dad didn't think much of them either. He said a lot of their stories were biased bullshit—short on facts and long on politics. He detested journalistic standards everywhere."

David raised his glass. "He could be difficult at times, but my dad had integrity."

"He wasn't afraid to go wherever a story took him. I hope he didn't get killed over it."

"Killed!"

Irene poured herself another drink. "Yeah, about six weeks ago a couple of guys in suits showed up at two in the morning and let themselves in your dad's place. They thought they were sneaky, but I watched through my front window curtains. My lights were out, so they didn't think I was up. They didn't leave till around four that morning. I thought about getting the police, but they felt like cops, or maybe out-of-town cops. You know, way too dressed-up for crooks in this neighborhood. Could be those guys or friends of theirs had something to do with Nick's disappearance. I'm sorry I said kill."

David looked around. "It doesn't look like there's much to steal. You've been here before. Is anything missing?"

Irene staggered with a half-empty shot glass and shoved her head in the bedroom. "Nothing is out of place." She slumped back on the couch and propped her feet on the coffee table.

Her white tennis shoes were dirty and worn, and her oversized lavender sweater had several small holes. But, those dark-green eyes still had vibrancy.

David learned Irene arrived in the Village in the Sixties from a small town in Ohio. Never married and now seventy-two, she lamented the change that had taken over her neighborhood the last twenty years.

Irene raised her voice. "This used to be an artists' community. You didn't need much to live and explore your craft—we were happy. Now you got to have a lot of money to get a half-decent place around here."

They talked for another hour, and then David helped Irene back to her home.

As they reached the door, Irene said, "I'll get Beau. He's anxious to go home. Your dad said Beau was fifteen, but he could pass for six or seven. Not a touch of gray in that long black hair, and his white spots are perfect. He still has the bouncy speed of a young cat. And, man is he feisty. He only weighs ten-pounds, but a couple of weeks ago he kicked the crap out of a big tomcat twice his size. He's smart and doesn't back down."

Irene refused payment for her time or the cans of cat food she gave David.

Beau ran around poking and pawing, getting reacquainted with his home. David pulled the First Communion picture out of the box, held it for a moment, and then set it on the coffee table along with a picture of his mom and dad on their wedding day. He tossed the rest of the stuff out.

While putting away the almost empty bottle of scotch it occurred to him his dad always kept a journal. It wasn't in the box from work, or sitting out anywhere. He knew his dad never stored that kind of personal stuff in an electronic device. He wondered if his dad had it with him when he disappeared.

David looked at Beau, and laughed. "Beau, where did my dad keep his journal?" Beau jumped up on the couch and wagged his tail.

"Come on, Beau, show me where it is."

Beau ran into the bedroom and clawed away at a spot on the oak floor under the bed. David pushed the bed aside and felt the loose floorboard. He pried up a couple of boards with a screwdriver and found a black leather-bound book about six inches wide and ten inches tall. David thumbed through a few pages and recognized his dad's hand writing. The journal might hold clues to his dad's disappearance.

It was around seven o'clock; David went out and picked up hamburgers and two sixteen- ounce containers of coffee. Twenty-five minutes later he was poring over the pages. There were reflections on his mom and the old days. David was surprised and touched by how often his dad mentioned their relationship, his little league teams and summer camps. There was even poetry about birds and flowers.

Peters said his dad made his first trip down to Tennessee back in May, so David scanned the document till he found several entries that seemed to start the story.

May 10th: *Clifford Hogan claims God told him that He intervened in the last presidential election. God picked the winner! Conversation supposedly took place under a weeping willow tree. What's the story? Where is Utopia, Tennessee?*

May 12th: *Talked Peters into sending me to Utopia. He thinks this is social media bullshit, but my gut says there's more to it.*

May 20th: *Interviewed Hogan—he's a good guy. Saw the weeping willow tree. I was surprised to find the FBI and other government people at that out of the way place. They employed their usual heavy handed tactics—I made a list. I don't know what to make of Hogan's story, but the FBI hauled him to Washington. I met an old girlfriend, Glenda Summers, in Utopia. She's covering the story for the Johnson City Sentinel. She looked great—maybe I'll give her a call.*

David tossed the empty coffee container in the wastebasket, made a quick trip to the bathroom, and started reading again.

May 27th: *Attended a circus event at the Dirksen Building in D.C. The ringmasters were Senator Shoults and Special Prosecutor Miller. Also in attendance were arrogant clowns from some of the major media outlets. Impression—they plan to stomp this story out. No sign of Hogan, word is the FBI has him stashed somewhere in town. I'm sure those bastards are giving him a "going over."*

June 4[th:] *A jerk named Harry Jones, one of Special Prosecutor Miller's gang, presided over a ridiculous event at the Dirksen Building. He dared God to show up and corroborate Hogan's story. The FBI dragged Hogan out and sat him in the front of the room. The old man looked like they beat the hell out of him. What's happened to America? I'll make sure they pay for this.*

June 12[th:] *The story has dropped out of sight. Nothing on social media or anywhere else, and Hogan has vanished. My contact at the Bureau said Hogan might have been taken out to Colorado, but he won't elaborate. Peters wants me back in New York, and told me to forget about this. I don't intend to let this go. But for now it's New York and local crime and politics.*

August 4[th:] *Hounded Peters into letting me take one more shot on this story. Next week I'll interview everyone in that hamlet. They know something. It's back to Utopia and the weeping willow mystery.*

August 4th was the last entry.

David closed the journal and looked at Beau. "What should we do?"

Social media no longer mentioned this story. David figured the powers that be must have pulled the old conversations and blocked any new ones.

He shrugged his shoulders. "Let's sleep on it, Beau. We can figure this out tomorrow."

It was a little past nine o'clock, Tuesday morning. David lay on the bed staring at a photo on the wall of his mom in her wedding dress and thinking of those lost ten years with his dad.

David showered, slipped into his jeans, and put on his dad's gray-cotton bathrobe. He then poured the rest of the scotch into a small glass, and settled down on the couch with the journal.

He reread the entry of May 20th, and looked at Beau. "Talking to Dad's old girlfriend Glenda Summers is our next logical step. She was in Utopia, and close with Dad at one time. Maybe Dad called her. She might be able to help us."

David grabbed his iPhone and looked up numbers in Johnson City, Tennessee. He found Glenda's, and one for the *Johnson City Sentinel*. He reached Glenda at work, brought her up to date on his dad's disappearance. They agreed to meet Thursday evening. From New York, it was a little over six-hundred miles to her apartment on Cherry St. He'd take I-78 and then I-81 S the rest of the way—about a ten-hour drive. He also called Pat's Saloon in Chicago and told his boss to find a permanent replacement.

Around eleven o'clock, Irene showed up in wrinkled jeans with a bright-orange stocking cap pulled over her shoulder-length gray hair. "You want to get something to eat?"

David grabbed his Chicago blue baseball cap. "Sure, let's go."

Irene looked at David's cap. "New Yorkers hate the Chicago teams almost as much as they hate the team from Boston."

"Hate is the poison of choice these days."

Irene nodded. "Hate is great at tearing things down, but it never builds anything."

Near the corner of Waverly and 7th Avenue, Irene pointed at a single-story white brick building. A neon sign above the entrance blazed BREAKFAST BEAT in bright red. "That's been here since the good old days. It never closes, not for New Year's, Christmas, or anything."

"Whew. It's a little beat up."

"It's seen a lot, that's part of its charm. Back in the day you could stop by at three in the morning, eat a big plate of scrambled eggs, drink tons of coffee loaded with sugar, and listen to poetry or someone share gritty details from their latest screenplay. That was exciting, and the energy carried a lot of wisdom. Now you never know when someone might flare up because you used the wrong word, supported the wrong candidate, or took the wrong position on anything. Hate has become cool, it shows you care. It didn't used to be that way."

"Do you want to go somewhere else?"

"No, we'll grab my window booth and not talk to anyone. That way we avoid any scenes. Besides, they still serve the best scrambled eggs."

As David pushed open the door, he was greeted with greasy bacon and sausage odors, and stares from a number of the diners.

Irene led them to a booth facing 7th Avenue. The booth had several patches over its faded blue plastic cover and dings and dents in the wooden table.

David ran his hand over *Irving 1958* carved deep into the table. "I wonder where this guy ended up. Think he got published, or acted on Broadway? Maybe he ran out to Hollywood and got his screenplay made into a blockbuster movie. Perhaps he ended up driving a cab in Jersey."

Irene tossed her stocking cap on the table, and smiled. "A lot of dreams. I hope his came true—mine didn't."

"Dreams and time seem to get away from all of us."

Irene gazed at the 7th Avenue hustle—waves of yellow cabs, honking horns, pointing, shouting, shoving—greed in a hurry.

After a few minutes, she said, "You used to be able to smoke in here. The air got so thick the smell clung to you for a week. That smell told people you had been somewhere and learned something. Light up now and you get arrested and sued in the bargain."

David looked around the diner. "I'm hungry. Do they take this long to show you a menu?"

Irene waved at a couple of servers near the check-out counter. "There's Julie and Fred. I'll get them over here."

The servers turned and faced the cash register.

A minute later Cybil, the manager, walked over and pointed to David's baseball cap. "I just got off the phone with the owner, and she told me not to serve anyone who supports that Chicago team."

David took off his cap. "If it bothers people, I'll lay it here in the booth out of sight, and won't put it back on till I'm outside."

"It's way too late for that. I know what that cap means, our employees know, and these customers know who you support. You got to leave before it gets ugly."

Cybil wagged her finger at Irene. "You brought this guy here, which means you tolerate what that cap represents. The owner told me to bar you in the future. Your kind doesn't belong in here."

Several patrons shouted at them to leave. At the next table, a young man tossed a half-eaten sausage link that struck Irene in the forehead.

David handed Irene her stocking cap, and said, "I'll slug that guy, and then we'll leave."

"No, I'll take care of him." She wiped the greasy stain off her face, and then dumped the young man's plate of scrambled eggs in his lap.

His dad's journal mentioned Saint Joseph's Parish on East 8th Street. Its red-brick tower and white pillars had been a Greenwich Village landmark since 1829. Wednesday morning, David hiked the three blocks and introduced himself to its pastor Father Paul.

Father Paul glanced toward the first row of pews. "Every Sunday morning at our seven o'clock mass your dad would light a candle and then take a seat over there. I can picture him in his tan suit holding a prayer book and singing the Our Father. We've missed him."

"Dad loves to sing. Seven o'clock Sunday morning was our family's mass time."

"He helped deliver food to shut-ins. Last August he stopped coming to Sunday services. After a couple of weeks I phoned and got no answer. I dropped by his home and ran into a lady named Irene, who said Nick was out of town on an important story. Now you say he's disappeared."

"August was the last time anyone had contact with him."

Father Paul put his hand on David's shoulder. "Sorry I can't provide any helpful information. Your dad was generous with his time and resources. I'll read his name at mass next Sunday and ask everyone to keep him in their prayers. I won't mention he's disappeared."

As he left, David shoved fifty dollars in the St. Vincent de Paul collection box.

Around eight-thirty Wednesday evening, David packed the journal in his suitcase, tucked Beau under his arm, and headed toward his car.

Irene ran up. "I hope you find your dad. He's a good man."

David kissed her on the cheek. "I'm headed to Tennessee. There's a lady down there that might be able to help me. Take care of yourself, and stay out of fights."

"David, it's a shame what's become of this town. I'm past grieving, and screaming never does any damn good. I've decided to get out. I don't want to die here."

"Where will you go?"

"Wherever there are good poets, smoky rooms, and dreams come true."

After several stops along the way, David arrived in Johnson City at two in the afternoon, Thursday. He checked in to a motel near the highway, fed Beau, and then got some hamburgers and a soda for himself.

Around seven o'clock, as Beau watched a nature show on TV, David headed to Glenda's place.

David hit a large pot hole and swerved to avoid others as he drove down Cherry Street, stopping at 221. She would be on the second floor-apartment B. He gazed at the worn brick buildings and older cars. Two of the four lights in the parking lot were out.

David recalled his dad's journal described Glenda as a sharp, no-nonsense reporter with an Ivy League education. Full of fun but always committed to facts and whatever truth they led to. It was clear his dad liked and admired her.

Glenda opened the door and stared a moment. "You look just like your dad. Come in, David."

On the right was a flat screen TV propped up on a metal stand, a coffee table, a green cloth-couch, and worn easy chair. Fifteen feet to the left was a stove, refrigerator, and a few cabinets, and straight ahead a curio cabinet with four glass shelves. A few pictures hung on the wall. The tan carpet showed several large stains.

Glenda closed the door. "Toss your jacket somewhere and grab a seat on the couch. I'll get us a drink, and then we'll talk. Is scotch and water OK?"

"Throw in ice."

David glanced over as Glenda prepared the drinks. She was tall, at least five-foot ten. His dad's journal gave her age as forty-six, but she could pass for ten years younger. Everything was tight, no fat—no loose skin.   No gray in that shoulder-length brunette hair. She looked great in jeans.

Glenda brought over the drinks and the bottle. "I last saw your dad in May, in that little oasis called Utopia. Since that's where he was supposed to be in August, that's where we'll start to look. It's about forty miles south of here."

David took a drink. "They found his rental in Memphis outside a strip club, and his credit cards used there."

"That's bullshit. But it says his disappearance was no accident."

"Why not start to look in Memphis?"

"The trail won't lead to Memphis. That's misdirection."

David set his glass down. "The FBI and state police have stopped looking."

Glenda leaned back on the couch. "I admired your dad. If he went back to Utopia in August it's because that's where the story was. It was a crazy story. Some guy said God talked to him about the presidential election. No journalists were there other than your dad, and me and my partner Phil. When we got back my editor at the *Sentinel* told me to forget the crackpot story. We never published it. I do know they took the guy who made the claim, his name was Hogan, to Washington and then a few weeks later the whole thing just died everywhere. I didn't think about it until you called."

"Who took this guy Hogan to Washington?"

"Phil and I watched the FBI shove that guy in a car and drive off. Your dad saw it too."

"Let's take a look at the pictures and recording you made."

Glenda finished her drink and stared at the empty glass. "None were ever taken. The FBI had a loop thrown around that little hamlet.

You had to drop off your cellphones, cameras, and recorders if you wanted to get in there to interview Hogan."

"You let them get away with that?"

"I was pissed. I called my boss and he said to go along with it. Sure it was crap, but not worth the fight if my boss wouldn't back me. Hell, it was a little place buried in the middle of nowhere. I couldn't figure out why the FBI and other government officials gave a shit. But your dad must have smelled something. He's the best damn journalist I've ever known."

"Why don't we call Phil, and get him over here. He might have seen something you forgot or overlooked."

"Phil died in an accident about six weeks ago. They found his car at the bottom of a ravine. An autopsy said he was loaded with drugs. I never knew Phil to take drugs, but we figured there's always that first time. No one suspected anything."

Glenda walked over to the curio cabinet. "Take a look at my bobble-head collection of saints. There's Saint Agnes, and next to her is Saint John, then there's good old Saint Christopher. I'm missing Saint Jude—the saint of desperate causes. Your dad wore a Saint Jude medal around his neck the whole time I knew him."

"He was never without it."

Glenda named the other saints in her collection, and then sighed. "With Phil dead and your dad disappeared, that just leaves me. I didn't see any other journalists down there. Damn!"

David refilled the glasses. "Don't worry, we'll take my car and drive down tomorrow and see what the people of Utopia might know about all this."

Glenda took a deep breath. "You mean all twelve including the kids. There were a couple of dogs, but they won't have much to say."

"I wonder if the FBI is still snooping around down there."

"I don't care. They won't get in my way. I didn't tell my boss about you, and I won't unless we find something the *Sentinel* might report. For now it's just me and you."

"It's me, you, and Beau."

"Who the hell is Beau?"

David turned as he walked out the door. "Beau is my dad's cat. He insisted on coming along. Back in New York I could tell he wanted to get to the bottom of this."

"Any friend of your dad is welcome. I love cats."

It was seven-thirty, Saturday morning; wearing a red cotton-plaid shirt and baseball cap, David was on his way to pick up Glenda.

At a stoplight, he glanced over at Beau. "Be nice to Glenda. She's a friend of Dad's, and will help us discover what happened."

Beau nodded, and then curled up and went to sleep.

Glenda, in jeans and wearing a light-blue jacket, was standing outside her apartment holding a large tan wicker basket.

She smiled. "I've packed a lunch. It's about forty miles and as rural as you can get."

Beau jumped into the back seat.

David said, "I couldn't find this Utopia online—GPS never heard of it. You'll have to give me directions."

"I'm not surprised. It's just a handful of broken-down buildings in the middle of the woods. But I remember the people being nice and gentle—real down-to-earth folks."

The dash read fifty-eight degrees.

Glenda rolled down the window. "This is my favorite season; it's that first frost mixed with a dash of color and woodsy bouquet. Fall makes everything feel, smell, and even taste better."

David nodded as Beau stared out the back window.

After thirty-five miles, Glenda pointed at a two-lane black-top. "Get on that road. Utopia is another five miles or so."

David looked around. "Man, you weren't kidding when you said rural. There's no cars or farms—just thick woods. Daniel Boone would love it here."

Glenda noted as they passed a large boulder on the right, "It's about a mile ahead."

They drove another two or three miles, and Glenda said, "Pull over!"

"What's the problem?"

"This is the right road, but where are the people, the dogs, and the buildings? Where's Utopia?"

"A place can't vanish in six months."

"This one did."

"I'll turn around and go back."

After a mile, Glenda saw a clearing. "Park there and we'll look around."

They climbed a small grassy hill and gazed at a forest of green, red, and yellow clinging to trees and bushes, the ground carpeted with decaying leaves and discarded branches. Four deer foraged in a small gully about a hundred yards away on the other side of the road. Beau watched a couple of gray squirrels loaded with acorns scamper up an oak tree. Nature was preparing its change of seasons.

With her hands on her hips, Glenda glanced around. "I'm not crazy. Those people and buildings were here."

"Nature can't swallow things that fast. If this is the right place, then something else got to it."

David watched Beau follow a rabbit down an overgrown path a few yards away. "Let's see where Beau is heading, maybe he's on to something."

As she ran along the path, Glenda looked back at David and laughed. "Good thing we wore jeans and tennis shoes. Hurry up old man."

The path emptied into a clearing about half the size of a football field, bordered on one side by a clear, fast moving creek, and on the other sides with thick stands of oaks, maples, poplars and green, brown and gold shrubs.

Glenda was standing near the creek when David arrived.

Breathing heavy, David bent over, and said, "I ain't used to this. Fell a couple of times back there. Have you seen Beau?"

Glenda scooped up a handful of the clear creek water. "Nope, just saw a few rabbits that scattered into the bushes when I got here. Oh yes, a cardinal has been hanging around."

She looked at a large oak tree on the other side of the creek. "See it pace back and forth on that branch. He's an anxious fellow, like he's been waiting for someone. "

David glanced around. "Damn, where did Beau get to?"

"He'll show up. Meanwhile, let's figure out our next move."

The cardinal pecked away at a knot high up in the oak tree. In a minute it had pulled something out and held it in its beak. It flew over and dropped its package.

David unfolded a wadded piece of paper. "It's my dad's handwriting."

To whom it may concern. Utopia has been razed. The people behind that are pursuing me. Twisted my leg—can't run. Get word to Jake Peters at the Journal. Nick Cyrus—journalist. August 11.

David wiped a tear as he shoved the note in his pocket. The cardinal watched from a nearby oak tree, and then disappeared in the woods.

Glenda said, "Who would have the power to rub out even a small place like Utopia?"

David tossed a rock at the creek. "I met my dad's boss on Monday. He doesn't give a damn about my dad. No point going there."

"The *Sentinel* dropped the story back in May, but this note and the disappearance of Utopia might get them interested."

"Can we prove Utopia ever existed? You don't have any before pictures, and the story has been erased from social media."

Beau scrambled from under a button bush dragging a small metal chain, his black fur covered in white petals. He dropped the chain at David's feet.

David dipped the chain in the creek, wiped it off with his shirt sleeve, and then held it up. "This is my dad's Saint Jude medal. He would never take this off."

Glenda squeezed David's shoulder. "That's too bad, you want to look around?"

"I do."

David slid the medal around his neck, and then brushed the petals off Beau's coat. "Where did you find this medal?"

Beau, along with two small gray squirrels, scampered toward a red patch of burning bushes two-hundred feet away. David grabbed a stick and began stabbing the ground and slashing the bushes.

Glenda said, "You look in this area, and I'll check the other side of the creek. Call out if you find anything."

The tree-top chatter of cardinals, blue jays, and goldfinches accompanied Glenda as she searched along the muddy creek bed. After a few hundred feet, she climbed up the grassy bank and ran into a big orange-bellied squirrel sitting on a rock gnawing away at an acorn. Later, while cutting through a patch of bright-yellow daisies, Glenda discovered a family of grayish-brown cottontails had begun to follow her.

When a breeze ushered in a minty scent, Glenda closed her eyes and pictured hummingbirds dancing with bees while sugar-plum fairies and snow-white angels held hands and watched from the nearby bushes and trees.

At a clearing in the woods, she climbed a small mound and gazed at a large blue lake sparkling in the distance.

Glenda was back after an hour, and said, "I didn't find any clues to your dad's disappearance."

David shrugged his shoulders. "Me neither. No clothing, bones, or shallow grave. Dad might be alive—I don't know. But he would never part with his St. Jude medal."

"We'll have lunch and talk. I'll run back to the car and get the basket. There's a perfect place on the other side of the creek."

A few minutes later, Glenda guided David and Beau to a grassy hilltop right above the creek. A tall oak tree provided shade, and a couple of tree stumps served as chairs.

Beau devoured a can of beef stew, while a rabbit with her four kittens huddled under a nearby mulberry tree. A few feet away, water splashed over and around rocks as the creek hurried toward its rendezvous with the lake.

Glenda handed David a cup of iced tea, a ham-on-rye sandwich, and a salad. "I didn't take a close look the first time I was here. But, God, this is paradise. I could live here year-round in a cabin or even a tent. I'd be away from that noise and hate out there."

David shook his head. "You can't get away. They won't let you. That's why Utopia is no longer around and my dad has disappeared. They have to be in charge of everything—even paradise."

"Last time I was here FBI and folks from the Special Prosecutors office were pushing people around. They got the power to make places and even ideas disappear."

David took a bite of his sandwich. "Look at all the junk that's been coming out about them—at least those at the top. But, I never figured they played this rough."

"Ten years ago they weren't, but times have changed. Anything is possible these days."

A fat box turtle walked off with a piece of discarded lettuce. A moment later a small gray squirrel dropped an acorn in Glenda's lap and then dashed up a nearby oak tree. David gave the left-over salad to the family of rabbits waiting under the mulberry tree.

Glenda reached into the basket. "Time to open the wine. I brought a zinfandel."

They sipped the sweet red and listened to a chorus of blue jays sing.

David leaned over and refilled Glenda's glass, and said, "Dad mentioned you a lot in his journal."

She brushed back her dark hair and smiled. "I feel like singing." She ran her hand through the thick grass. "They say touch has a memory."

Thirty minutes later the bottle was empty.

Walking back to the car, they gazed at a swaying field of white lilies.

Glenda said, "Look at those lilies dance. Next spring we'll venture down to the lake…maybe take a swim."

David set the basket down as they emerged from the woods. A blue sedan was parked twenty feet behind his Jeep. Leaning against the sedan's passenger side door was a thin, gray-haired man dressed in a charcoal colored suit, white shirt, and bright-red tie. He was about five-foot eight, and with that pale complexion looked at least sixty to David.

The man stomped out his cigarette. "David, Glenda, let's talk."

Beau watched from behind a log.

Glenda yelled, "Who are you? Talk about what?"

The man flashed a gold badge stamped with Federal Bureau of Investigation. "Josh Levitt. Here's my photo ID."

They shook hands, and then Josh glanced at the log. "We even know about Beau over there."

David shoved the basket in the back seat. "If you know so much—where's my dad?"

Glenda stood next to the Jeep's front passenger door. "Where's Utopia?"

Josh nodded. "We'll talk about Nick Cyrus and Utopia, and a lot more. A few miles out of Johnson City there's a motel on Hwy-19W, called the Vanity Inn. I'm in room 26. Let's meet there at eight o'clock tonight. I'll fill you in about what's going on."

Josh shouted as he walked to his car. "You got to trust somebody in this fucking world."

As the sedan drove off, David looked at Glenda. "Trust him?"

"Finding truth can be risky. We've got to meet this guy and see where it leads."

Beau jumped on Glenda's lap, and they pulled away.

They arrived at Glenda's around five thirty. GPS put the Vanity Inn at a fifteen minute drive.

Glenda tossed a frozen pizza in the microwave, set a couple of cans of root beer on the counter, and said, "I've got to get something."

A short while later Glenda walked out of the bedroom. "My 38 Special is gone. It was there this morning. I bought it a few years ago for protection. There are break-ins all the time around here. I kept it loaded and ready under a nightgown in my dresser drawer."

David sliced the pizza. "That's the kind of thing crooks would steal. Is it registered?"

"It's registered. Damn, I was planning on bringing it tonight—just in case."

"What else is missing?"

"All my saints are here, just the gun was taken. Whoever did it was very neat about it, nothing torn up in there. The timing seems strange."

"Do you still want to go tonight?"

"We got to."

It was seven-forty. From a gas station across the highway, David, Glenda, and Beau watched the neon sign VANITY MOTEL flash its gold letters. The motel rooms were stacked in two rows of thirteen. The parking lot contained two pickup trucks, an old Volkswagen bus, and the sedan. Other than the management office, the only light on was on the second floor at the far end near where the sedan was parked.

Ten minutes passed, and David said, "It's almost too quiet."

"Yeah. I wish I had my gun."

"Hell, let's get this over with. Like the man said, you have to trust someone in this fucking world."

"We'll listen and then decide how much trust to put in this guy."

They parked just outside Room 26, and agreed to take turns watching out the window for any activity near the Jeep.

Still in suit and tie, Josh smiled, and thanked them for coming. David sat in a chair nearest the door, Glenda on a small brown couch near the window. After exploring the place, Beau snuggled next to Glenda.

Josh gave Beau a treat, and then lit a cigarette. "I've been with the Bureau almost thirty years. Plans are to retire in a couple of months. I'm glad to get out. I've had so many arguments with my bosses over the stuff going on I'm sure they're happy to be rid of me."

Josh walked to the counter. "I've got a bottle of scotch."

Glenda nodded. "Sounds good."

David peeked through the blinds. "I'll take mine with ice."

Josh handed out the drinks, and then tossed Beau another treat. "Both of you are on the Bureau's watch list. Glenda, since you went down to Utopia that first time. David, from the day you arrived in New York. Your dad's place was bugged, and the Bureau learned you found his journal. I'm not in charge of that operation, but I have a friend who brought me up to date. We're a small group, but there's a mutiny underway within the Bureau to all this stuff. My friend told me you were heading here, so I took a week vacation, and watched Glenda's apartment until you showed up. Then I followed you guys at a distance down to Utopia."

Glenda said, "Utopia's gone."

"The Bureau used one of their special contractors to do that work. They brought in a crew from across the border, and when they finished they shipped the workers back home. The whole operation took less than two days and left no witnesses to what happened. Everything was fine until your dad showed up."

"Is my dad still alive?"

"My friend says Nick is being held in Colorado. That he and others are locked up in some old mining town twenty miles outside of Aspen. An American Gulag by any other name."

Glenda glanced out the window. "That sounds crazy."

"They take care of anyone who might be a threat to the Deep State."

Josh took off his jacket and poured another round of drinks. "What I'm about to share gets even harder to believe.

"Twelve years ago the Bureau wanted to speed up the wheels of justice when it came to so-called terrorists and organized crime figures. So the folks at the top decided to have those bad boys killed or disappear—same thing. The secret program was code-named The Liquidation File. That's a list you don't want to be on.

"In the beginning I was ok with the program because it was getting rid of genuine bad guys and saving American lives. But after a couple of years it began targeting activists, actors, industrialists, even some politicians were showing up as suicides, in car accidents, drug overdoses, and drownings. They caused a plane to crash in the side of a mountain to get rid of one passenger."

David got up, glanced out the window, and then stared at Glenda. "What the fuck are we up against?"

Josh took a drag on his cigarette. "You're up against the greatest threat to our freedom since the republic was founded."

Glenda borrowed a cigarette, and said, "Is it just big shots at the FBI running this program, or is there others involved?"

"The real power is behind the scenes—the FBI is just a tool."

"Who are these people behind the scenes?"

"Glenda, I don't have the list of names. But it would include high-level government bureaucrats, moneyed globalists, and one-world activists, among others. That's the Deep State."

"So using whatever criteria, these folks behind the scenes order a hit and the FBI carries it out."

"Not quite. Like when they got rid of Utopia, the Bureau contracts out this kind of specialized work. Names put on the Liquidation File are handled by a private group out of Los Angeles that works exclusively for the Bureau. They get the work done within sixty to ninety days, faster if it's a rush job.

"If the Deep State just wants to embarrass a target and force him or her out of the public square, they'll frame them up for something using fake documents or fake stories leaked to friends in the media. You know—fake news.

"But for things more serious, the Deep State might order up a suicide, which can include jumping from a building or off a cliff, hanging, drug overdose, gas, pills, they're lots of choices. They even got handwriting experts to forge the suicide note.

"Hell, that's just suicides. They produce accidents if it's decided to go that route. Things like car accidents, drownings, tumbling down a flight of stairs, the options here are endless, and a suicide note isn't needed.

"Sometimes people just fucking disappear. I don't have a name, but I heard the person in charge of fulfilling all Liquidation File contracts is a Hollywood producer who uses stuntmen, actors, and special effect people to pull these jobs off. I once heard the head of the Bureau say, 'get a hold of Jacob, this is a job for his team at *1984*.'"

Beau pulled at the blinds and then talked Josh into giving him another treat.

David refilled his glass and looked at Glenda. "I'm just an out-of-work actor and bartender looking for his dad. Now I'm facing something a hell of a lot bigger."

"We can't separate the two. Uncovering what happened to Nick will expose this other stuff. Things have gotten bigger, but I'm going after it. We have to defeat these bastards and I hope you're with me."

David raised his glass. "You're right, Glenda. We'll go where it takes us."

Josh chimed in. "That makes three of us. I also got friends in the Bureau that will help."

David looked at Beau. "He found my dad's journal and Saint Jude medal. I'm sure he wants in."

Josh tossed Beau another treat, and said, "Our next stop is somewhere in Colorado. I have a friend in the Bureau feeding me information on these things. I'll ask him for details on that mining town where your dad and others are supposedly being held. We can start unraveling this crap by exposing that operation.

"And, Glenda, don't bother taking this to the *Sentinel*. The Bureau got to your boss back in May when he told you to drop the story. That's why I didn't take this whole thing to other media outlets. I don't know who to trust in the media."

"OK—forget the *Sentinel*. What about my co-worker Phil? Was that Hollywood group responsible for his death?"

Josh shrugged. "I don't know. I'll text you guys tomorrow and we'll meet in Colorado next week."

As they pulled out of the parking lot, David said, "He seems to know a hell of a lot. But can we trust him?"

"We got to take a chance. He's the only game in town. But if he's lying we're screwed."

David looked in the back seat. "Beau, yell if you spot anyone following us."

Sunday afternoon Josh sent a text, telling them to meet him at the Annie Laurie Inn in Aspen for lunch on Tuesday. No other information was included. Glenda resigned from the *Sentinel* via a text.

Taking I-70, they left Monday morning in David's Jeep for the day's drive to Aspen.

Ten-thirty Tuesday, they checked in at the Mega Motel on W. Main St., and then met in David's room.

Glenda reached into her purse for a cigarette. "Josh tossed a lot of general information but few details we could use to strike a blow at the Deep State. We need facts that can be checked and proved."

"First we find out what happened to my dad. That's why we started all this."

"Sure, we'll push him on that. We also need more on the Liquidation File and that group out in Hollywood he referred to as *1984.*"

"Is that a code of some kind, maybe an address, or is there a larger meaning behind *1984*? What do you think?"

"Getting that answer will provide a clearer picture of all this. One thing we know—killing doesn't bother them."

David sat on the edge of the bed. "Josh said we were just on their Watch List."

"Maybe we got promoted to the Liquidation File. Let's head over and see what Josh has for us."

David turned as they walked out the door. "Beau, keep an eye on things while were gone."

David and Glenda arrived around twelve-fifteen at the Annie Laurie Inn on Hwy 13. In the surrounding hills, oaks, cottonwoods, and pines were wearing autumn orange, bright reds, shades of gold, and a few lingering greens. Canoes and small boats leisurely moved about the nearby lake while the midday sun bounced off the cool clear water. Crisp air carried the scent of decaying leaves and twigs.

The crowded terrace had twenty-five metal tables spaced ten-feet apart. From there you could gaze at the lake or take in the colorful hillside.

Josh, wearing jeans and gray sweatshirt, rose as they approached. "Doesn't this place take your breath away? My goodness—look at

that lake. It makes you forget how ugly things have gotten out there.
When I retire, I'll find a place like this and get away from it all."

A purple butterfly the size of a half dollar floated past in the
direction of the lake.

David glanced at the butterfly. "You can't beat nature for its love of
beauty. I was in this area a couple of summers back with my acting
troupe for a Shakespeare festival. We did an outdoor performance of
A Midsummer Night's Dream just on the other side of the lake near
that stand of cottonwoods."

Josh nodded. "Shakespeare!"

As he waved for a server, Josh said, "My friend in the Bureau says
he has a map that takes us to the location your dad and others are being
held, and he knows where he can get a copy of the Liquidation File."

Glenda asked, "What about that Hollywood group you referred to
as *1984*?"

"My friend said he would run down Jacob's last name."

A red-headed, freckled, thirtyish-looking man came over and took
their order. David and Glenda each got a deluxe burger with cheese, a
plate of jumbo fries, and a sixteen-ounce cola. Josh just wanted a
piece of pumpkin pie and coffee.

After the server left, Glenda asked, "When will we see this
information?"

"He'll bring it at six o'clock. I'm in room 117."

David asked, "What time do you want us to come by?"

"It might spook him if he found out you guys were involved. Come
at seven-thirty. My friend will be gone and I'll have the information."

Josh looked at David. "You said Shakespeare; that's great. What
role did you play in Midsummer?"

"Puck."

"The jester—the best part in the play."

"You bet; everyone wants to play that role. Next spring we're
bringing Chicagoland a new interpretation of Macbeth."

Josh smiled. "I'll come see you, I'll be retired then."

The food arrived. Josh took a drink of coffee and lit a cigarette. An
hour later, David and Glenda were heading to the parking lot.

On the way back to the motel, David looked at Glenda. "The guy that served our food, did he look familiar to you?"

"You mean that freckled guy. He stared at me with a weird grin while taking my order. But I've never seen him before. Why do you ask?"

"Seeing that guy bothered me, and I'm not sure why."

David and Glenda spent the rest of the afternoon watching a soccer game at Harry's, a sport's bar adjacent to the motel.

At seven-twenty, David and Glenda waited in the parking lot at the Annie Laurie Inn.

Glenda checked her cellphone. "That's strange, no text or email messages, and I've lost access to the Internet."

David grabbed his phone. "Mine is dead, too. What the hell is going on?"

"Let's go see Josh. The answer is probably waiting in room 117."

The door was ajar. David knocked several times and then shouted Josh's name.

David said, "Maybe he went out for cigarettes?"

"Let's go in."

Josh was slumped over on the couch; blood covered his face and sweatshirt.

Glenda felt his pulse. "He's dead. It looks like the Deep State has canceled our meeting. Wipe your fingerprints off the door knob. Let's get out of here."

"Shouldn't we ask management to call the police?"

"We're being set up, and I don't know who to trust. Let's get back to the motel, grab Beau, and just drive. That gives us time to figure what to do next."

Fifteen minutes later they were back at the motel. Glenda packed her suitcase while David waited at the door. They entered David's room and encountered an armed intruder.

Holding a 45, the intruder waved his hand. "Close the door."

Glenda grabbed David by the arm. "Isn't that the server from lunch?"

"Yeah, it looks like our freckled friend is moonlighting."

The intruder laughed. "I'm a stuntman that occasionally kills people for money. Being a server was just a role. Wasn't I good?"

David stepped toward the dresser. "I thought I recognized you. Have you had any speaking parts?"

"I was a bartender in the movie *The Dirty Five*. My line was 'What will you gents have?' A minute later my role ended in a hail of bullets."

"I've seen that movie a dozen times—you were great. I told Glenda I recognized you."

"Thanks, my mom loves that movie too. By the way, my name is Craig Spence."

Glenda lit a cigarette. "I'll put that movie on my bucket list."

Craig lowered the gun. "Don't make plans. After my friends get here, you guys and that Jeep end up over the side of a mountain. Careless driving while fleeing the murder you two just committed. You see, Josh was killed with the 38 Special we stole from your apartment. Your fingerprints are still on that gun registered to you, Glenda. At lunch I snapped a few pictures of the three of you together. I also took those water glasses you guys used and dropped them off in his room. Your fingerprints are all over those glasses, which will prove you were in the room. The local cops will find the gun where we planted it, and we'll create a motive that satisfies them. Two days from now I'll be back in LA."

David inched a little closer to Craig. "Can you tell me what happened to my dad Nick Cyrus?"

"Since you're such a big fan of my movie—Nick was liquidated last August. He was shot in those woods down in Tennessee, and dumped in the Pacific Ocean. It was a quick, clean liquidation."

David touched the St. Jude medal and lowered his head. Out of the corner of his eye he saw Beau approach Craig from behind. A few seconds later Beau ripped into Craig's right achilles tendon. As Craig swung around, David grabbed the large glass pitcher on the dresser and bashed him on the head.

Craig and the gun fell to the floor.

David grabbed the gun. "I ought to shoot this fucker. Let's go before his friends arrive."

Glenda went through Craig's pockets, taking his wallet and a large role of hundred-dollar bills. "Traveling money—it's the least he owes us."

David slid the gun in his waistband, kicked Craig in the ribs several times, and then scooped up Beau.

A minute later they were on Hwy 82 speeding out of town. After a half-hour and forty miles they pulled into a rest stop.

Glenda counted the money she had taken from Craig. "There's over twelve thousand bucks. His ID shows an address in Los Olivos, CA. That's a small town near Los Angeles."

David turned the engine off. "Have you got something in mind?"

"We're framed up good for Josh's killing. Our cellphones are dead, and so is Josh. The way out is for us to expose that Hollywood gang called *1984*."

"Where do we start?"

"The guy running it is a movie producer named Jacob. We know it's in Hollywood and that guy Craig works there. We also know that it employs people in the movie industry. Not a lot, but it's a start point. They can track credit card activity, so we'll use that cash to pay our way. I've got a friend from college that lives in LA. She'll put us up for as long as we need."

Glenda leaned over and hugged David. "We both loved your dad— he's irreplaceable. We have to make them pay for him, Josh, and what they're doing to our great country."

David kissed Glenda, and then looked in the back seat. "Beau, you saved our ass. In all this excitement I forgot to thank you. You've earned a bag of treats and then some."

Beau nodded and flicked his fluffy black tail. He then rolled on his back and went to sleep.

A rattle of thunder cut through the night air and a heavy rain began to pelt the Jeep.

David started up the engine, turned on the window wipers, and said, "LA, here we come."

A Call to Courage

"Courage is noble because it contributes to the well-being of the community"

Cicero had been an associate professor of philosophy at a Kansas junior college. After Gale his wife of twenty years died of cancer, he quit his job and took to the road in his old faded-green sedan. Over the last five years he had traveled from Absarokee, Montana, to Mount Carmel, Tennessee, and other small towns sharing the wisdom of Aristotle's writings on ethics and politics and the danger of totalitarianism from Orwell's *1984*.

He was fifty-five years old, six-foot tall, thin, with wavy gray hair. Besides jeans, tennis shoes, and a red or blue-plaid shirt, he always wore a light-tan baseball cap embossed across the bill in red letters with the word "freedom." His deep voice and engaging smile passionately argued good government principles and spread dark warnings to rural and working class communities.

In September, the Deep State decided that Cicero had become too dangerous and needed to be removed. The plan was simple. During his visit to Farmington, MO, in late October, Cicero would be abducted, drugged, and his car sent hurdling over a hillside. A local operative named Megan would befriend Cicero, and lure him to a location where the abduction team would be waiting. Megan had been doing clandestine work for the Deep State for ten years, ever since being recruited by the dean of the English department at the East Coast University she attended.

TUESDAY

Cicero arrived in Farmington early Tuesday morning and checked into Bonnie's Inn, a motel on the outskirts of town on old Hwy 67. There had been Internet buzz about his planned trip to Farmington, and his Saturday night discussion at the Big Barn. He never charged a fee, but donation buckets were passed among his audience.

Founded in 1822, Farmington was seventy-two miles southwest of St. Louis, in the lead belt region of Missouri. Not much had changed over the years in this community of sixteen thousand. Kathee's Malts had been on W. Liberty St. since 1961. Pap's Drugs was still the only drug store, and Masterson's Feed & Grain on E. Karsch always drew a Saturday morning crowd.

Cicero left his motel room for town around eleven o'clock. Sixty degrees and a slight breeze made it perfect sweater weather; the autumn air carried a scent of burnt leaves.

As Cicero strolled down First Street, he stopped at the Old Hobby Shop and studied the models in the display window. On the top shelf were plastic mummies, bloody werewolves, and vampires; below that were sports cars, U.S. battleships and German submarines from World War II—stuff he built as a kid. He was tempted to go in, but a rusty metal sign on the other side of the narrow street caught his attention; it read "Roscoe's Repairs."

Cicero ran over and entered the faded red-brick building jammed with big screen televisions, cameras, lawn mowers, power tools, a large crystal chandelier, even an old brass bed.

While Cicero looked over the repaired equipment, a short, bald elderly man in overalls walked out of a room in the back, followed by an overweight golden retriever. The dog glanced at Cicero, and then settled down on a worn green rug near the counter.

The man approached Cicero, and said, "I'm Roscoe and that's Goldie. Can we help you?"

Cicero shook the old guy's hand. "I noticed your sign and had to drop in and tell you it is great seeing things fixed rather than thrown out. When I was a kid if anything broke around the house my dad fixed it. That included our radios, televisions, even the plumbing. We changed brakes and water pumps on the family car right there in the driveway. In my growing-up neighborhood everybody did that. Your place reminds me of that spirit and energy."

"There's still enough of that around here to keep me in business. I sell a fair number of parts, but it's not like it used to be. A lot of folks just throw it out and buy new on credit. Debt doesn't seem to bother people, or for that matter our government anymore."

Cicero picked up a repaired power drill. "You're right. Many Americans have lost a sense of thrift and pride in the 'I can take care of it myself' attitude. Hard to believe how much things have changed since we were kids."

"And not for the better."

"Amen."

At twelve-thirty, Cicero held the door at Kathee's Malts for a woman and her two small children, and then followed them in. Straight ahead were four blue plastic booths against the wall and another four to the left. In the center of the room were two worn wooden tables, each with four chairs. To the right was a long soda-fountain bar packed with noisy teenagers sitting on twelve swivel chairs with bright red cushions. The floor was tiled pale white. Half-empty plastic catsup and mustard containers and a stack of white paper napkins sat on every table. Near the door was a big orange jukebox belting out music from long ago. Hanging on the walls were pictures of rock-and-roll bands from the Fifties and Sixties.

Cicero grabbed the last empty booth. A few minutes later a server named Claudette walked over.

He tossed his freedom cap on the table, and said, "Please give me two well-done fat burgers loaded with pickles, onions, and smother it all with cheddar cheese. Add fries and supersize my chocolate shake."

Claudette pointed at Cicero's cap. "Now there's a precious word—freedom. America doesn't treat it with enough respect these days. Take freedom of speech, people are getting afraid to speak up and share their thoughts. Shout freedom and some brand you a troublemaker. Mister, are you a troublemaker?"

"Some say I am. But, I don't mind trouble in the name of freedom."

"Amen."

While Cicero waited, a server walked past with four candles atop a chocolate cake and set it in front of a little boy at a table in the middle of the room. As they lit the candles, Cicero walked over and joined the parents in singing happy birthday.

He had just finished his second fat burger when four teenage girls crowded around his booth; one leaned over, and said, "Are you Cicero?"

"That's me."

"We heard you were coming. Can I ask a question?"

"Go ahead."

"I just read Orwell's *1984*, and he kept repeating the formula 2+2=5. What did he mean by that?"

"That's the key insight of his great work. Totalitarian truth is whatever Big Brother, the Deep State, or the Power in charge says it is. One week it could be five, the following week the formula might conclude 2+2=3, and the next week seven. Facts and fiction are the same, and evidence to the contrary is irrelevant. A place where reason has no role."

"But people could still point out that 2+2 must equal 4."

Cicero shook his head. "Nope, a totalitarian run world doesn't allow challenge or dissent of any kind."

She looked at her friends, and laughed. "Totalitarian sounds like the name of a crime family."

"It's the worst kind of crime family. It's people running the state doing the lying, cheating, threatening, and denying freedoms. And because it's the state it's all legal. Totalitarians fear freedom because it exposes truth, and that makes it a challenge to their hold on power. That's why we need courageous people willing to fight for freedom."

A young woman in the next booth shouted. "What's so important about truth?"

Cicero rose. "Justice requires truth! Economics requires truth! Democracy requires truth!"

Someone yelled, "What about greater truths?"

Cicero laughed. "That's a damn myth. Truth doesn't have rank order and it's not exclusive to one group over another. Beware of people that arm themselves with 'greater' truths—they're dangerous."

Cicero glanced around the room. "Demand truthfulness from educators, media, the legal profession, politicians, and businesses. Demand truth from everyone—including yourself."

Claudette hugged Cicero. "It's a hard world, but at least we have you."

The malt shop erupted with applause as Cicero walked out the door.

Around two-thirty, Cicero was people watching on the front steps of the city's public library when a slender young woman in jeans with shoulder-length blond hair scooted next to him.

She stared with her dark blue eyes, and said, "My name's Megan. I listened back at the malt shop—you were great. Your comments were so powerful in light of what's going on these days."

"It was mostly Orwell's wisdom. Have you read *1984*?"

"Not yet, but I plan on getting the book."

"It's a great read. The totalitarian threat is out there, the Communists of the twentieth century or the Deep State today. There are always people who want to control our lives."

Megan leaned against Cicero, and said, "Why is there so much hate?"

"Totalitarianism survives on hate and fear. There has to be someone to envy and blame for the lack of this or the breakdown of that. But, you never know when the finger of hate will be pointed at you for being with the wrong people, or misstating something, or appearing to support the wrong anything. Hate generates fear and then terror—that keeps everyone in line. In *1984* Orwell describes an activity called 'hate week' where everyone is regularly reminded by Big Brother who the current enemy is."

"Who is this Big Brother?"

"It's a term Orwell used for those in charge of a totalitarian world where no one can ever be happy. Today the Deep State wants the same kind of control."

Megan whispered, "Do you think the Deep State might be after you?"

"I've had my tax returns audited the last three years, and I found out the FBI went to my old employer and demanded a copy of my personnel file."

"But why are you doing things that anger the powerful?"

"After my wife died, I decided to commit myself to helping preserve our rights and freedoms for the next generation. Our country depends on those freedoms, and they're being eroded. I'm fighting today so we don't end up in Orwell's world tomorrow. I hope the powerful are upset, that means I'm having success."

Cicero took off his cap and smiled. "Megan, do you live around here?"

"I'm from Knob Lick, about nine miles south of here, and work at the correctional center here in Farmington. I went to college out East and majored in the Romantics—Keats, Byron, Shelley."

"Keats! Great poetry always has something important to say."

Cicero picked up a discarded soda can and tossed it in a nearby yellow trash barrel. "I'll be strolling around the city till Saturday evening. Maybe we'll bump into each other again."

"I'm sure we will."

Megan waved as Cicero headed toward his car, and then called her boss in Washington.

A high-pitched woman's voice answered. "How is it going?"

"I've made contact. He's alone, and will be here till Saturday evening. Send some folks. By the time they arrive I should have an idea of the best time and place to snatch him. This should be easy."

"A team will be there Friday morning. Have you learned anything?"

"Yeah, Cicero loves poetry."

THURSDAY

Thursday morning, Cicero was passing Sandi's Candy & Coffee Shop when the dark chocolaty scent and aroma of fresh-brewed coffee became irresistible. He bought a plate of assorted sweet chocolates and a sixteen-ounce espresso and sat at a wooden table next to the floor-to-ceiling white-stone fireplace at the center of the room. Oak planks scuffed from years of use covered the floor. Recessed lights in the ten-foot ceiling provided a soft glow, while friendly chatter and heat from the fireplace gave the room a warm cozy feel.

Cicero ate a couple of dark chocolates loaded with pecans, and then closed his eyes.

A few minutes passed, and then a voice said, "Do you mind if I sit down?"

Cicero looked up. "It's nice to see you again, Megan."

As she slung her light-blue jacket on the back of the chair, she said, "I drop by here all the time to munch on the dark chocolates and relax."

"When do you go to work?"

"I'm off this week, and just planned on hanging around the city. Then I got lucky and met you. I learned so much the other day."

"You're too kind."

"I mean it. People clapped as you left the malt shop. You caused them to think and question things. We need more of that."

Cicero glanced at the door. Led by a short middle-aged woman, a dozen small children dressed in Halloween costumes marched in and grouped near the check-out counter. The place erupted with smiles and applause.

Megan said, "That's Mrs. Nifong and her second grade class. She's a sweet lady. The grade school is a couple of blocks from here. I went there when I was a kid. God, where does time go?"

Cicero recognized a couple of ghosts, angels and fairies, a cowboy, what looked like a pirate, and a little girl that was either a very shaggy dog or werewolf.

Cicero laughed. "One year my grandma dragged me around the neighborhood in a crazy duck costume. I toughened up the next year and went out as the Frankenstein Monster."

Megan clasped her hands. "I remember dressing as a fairy princess. It was an all-white costume with a sparkly red wand and gold halo. I got a lot of candy that year. Funny how you recall those things."

Mrs. Nifong lined the kids in two rows of six. They sang Halloween songs, and then closed with "God Bless America" to a standing ovation.

After the applause, a little girl dressed as an angel stepped forward, and said, "Knock, Knock…"

Everyone yelled. "Who's there?"

"Ben!"

"Ben who?"

"Ben waiting to get candy all day!"

She giggled and told several more jokes, and then bowed. Sandi the owner gave each of the kids a large bag of sweets.

Cicero watched the kids leave, and then turned to Megan. "That was beautiful. Sometimes I wish I could do it all over again—you know what I mean. I wonder what happened to my Frankenstein costume."

Megan grabbed Cicero's arm. "There's a little park next door. Let's finish our coffee there."

Cicero and Megan settled on a metal bench next to a patch of long-needled evergreen trees and gazed at the two acres of green space in the center of town. A warm breeze swept bright red, autumn orange, and faded green leaves across the lawn to the street where the wind pushed them scratching over the concrete pavement. A gray squirrel hurried up an oak tree gripping an acorn while blackbirds foraged near the drinking fountain.

Megan sipped her coffee, and said, "Who's in charge out there?"

Cicero surveyed the park. "Nature does a pretty good job sorting its things out."

"I meant our world."

"Then the question isn't who's in charge, but who should be in charge. The answer to that has a lot of layers to it."

"All right, who should be in charge?"

"A very wise man named Aristotle addressed the issue twenty-three hundred years ago."

"Is that relevant today?"

"Wisdom never grows old."

Megan leaned over. "What did that wise man have to say?"

"It starts with what we want from our political community. Is there a goal that makes sense to everyone? Aristotle proffered, 'that we all live well.'"

"Good luck on getting everyone to agree on what living well means."

"Agreement comes from our ability to exercise virtuous reason so we can distinguish just from unjust—having a common sense of fairness and justice. From there we get laws, people that administer the laws, and the kind of political leadership that maintains good government."

"It sounds so damn simple. How come everyone is at each other's throat these days?"

"That's easy, society's character needs work. Virtue has lost its way and taken noble and good with it."

"I guess we need to spend more time reading Aristotle and Orwell. I'll add that to my bucket list."

Cicero got up and stretched. "Reading is good, but you have to act on what you learn. We need to get society to change its bad habits by challenging what we know is wrong. That means confronting the powerful and the tools they have to keep you silent. It takes courage to stand up to the Deep State. Courage is my discussion topic Saturday night."

"I'll be there."

The afternoon sun poked through the tree branches as Cicero and Megan strolled around the park discussing their favorite Christmas movies. They watched two cottontails snuggle under a crabapple tree, and listened as a noisy flock of Canadian geese flew overhead.

Near the drinking fountain, Cicero stopped and took a deep breath. "Wow, that's pumpkin pie I smell."

Megan smiled. "That's coming from Maggie's Pies. She cooks fresh a couple times a day. We can get a warm slice of pie with a big scoop of home-made ice cream. It's just around the corner."

"Let's go."

FRIDAY

Friday morning, Megan pulled onto an isolated gravel road just off Route DD, and waited. Around ten-thirty a black Jeep rolled up and parked behind her. Four men dressed in military fatigues got out and approached, led by a tall heavy-set man with a bushy red beard and crew cut. The bearded man opened Megan's front passenger side door and sat across from her, while the other three crowded in the back seat.

He leaned across the front seat, and said, "I'm Red."

A little shaken, Megan responded, "It's nice to meet you and your friends."

"Lady, I don't have friends. The Deep State is paying us two-hundred thousand to get rid of this guy Cicero, and that's all. What I need is a time and place when he will be alone, or just with you."

Megan stared at the deep scars running across Red's forehead. "The best time will be Saturday night after he finishes his presentation on courage. He's been lent the use of a building, and about seventy-five to a hundred locals are expected to show up. He told me he's checking out right after he finishes. That should put him back at his motel room out on Hwy. 67 about fifteen minutes after the meeting wraps up. You can grab him there."

"You'll have to attend the meeting and give us a call as soon as it breaks up. We can't be there because some idiot with a cellphone might snap a picture of me or one of the guys in the back seat. I can't risk that, so we'll wait for your call and then head over to his motel room."

"OK."

Red grinned. "I noticed you admiring my pretty scars. I used to do some cage fighting, almost killed a guy. Now I kill people for a living. It's up to seventeen now, but none ever paid as much as this guy Cicero. They must want to shut him up real bad."

Megan gripped the steering wheel.

Red lit a cigarette and leaned back in the seat. "Megan, my first kill was a trouble-making minister down in Texas. Hell, I spread his righteous body parts all over that state."

From the back seat, Charlie shouted, "My first was a fat old lady from the Bronx, up there in New York. She was given a whole bunch of warnings to lay off the Deep State, but she just wouldn't shut the fuck up. We yanked her out of her wheelchair and tossed her down a flight of stairs. I can still see her bloody head bouncing and banging on those metal steps—God that was fun."

Red glanced at Charlie. "My favorite was this federal judge the Deep State worried might someday get nominated to the Supreme Court. We caught him during the summer at his vacation home up in Montana. He was fishing while his wife and kids were out shopping. My partners held him under water while I beat him with a rock above his right eye. That made it look like he slipped and hit his head and drowned. They found his body about a half mile downstream. It was listed as an accidental drowning. I bought a new car with the money I earned on that one."

Red took a drag and then flicked his cigarette butt out the window. "Enough of this memory lane shit. Everybody knows what they have to do."

As he got out of the car, Red turned and stared at Megan. "Don't fuck up."

After they drove off, Megan walked to a nearby patch of woods and leaned against an oak tree and gazed up at the sweet autumn reds and quiet golds clinging for life from its branches. She had helped the Deep State embarrass people, even got some folks fired. But, she had never been involved with someone's murder. She was caught between respect and affection for Cicero and her fear of a lunatic named Red.

Leaves suddenly filled the air, shook loose from their branches by a gust of wind. Megan looked around, saw a rock and flung it as far as she could.

SATURDAY

Everyone still called it the Big Barn; it was near the edge of town just off Weber Road. Owned by a prosperous farm family named Mesey, the barn had been converted to a twenty-five thousand square foot brick and steel warehouse and office building years ago. Dan Mesey had granted Cicero use of the space for Saturday evening.

Megan arrived at the Big Barn around six-twenty, and parked near the door. It was a cold mid-forties with heavy rain predicted for later that night.

An old man in green overalls held the metal door as Megan walked in. There were already a few people sitting in the hundred or so metal folding chairs spread in five rows on the concrete floor. Megan recognized a couple from Knob Lick. She unzipped her gray parka and slung it over the back of a chair in the front row, and then walked to a large metal table with bowls of candy and free coffee.

Over the next forty minutes individuals, couples, and families trickled in. A few were holding copies of Orwell's *1984*. Around six-fifty, Mrs. Nifong, bundled in a big black overcoat, entered and sat in the second row with her husband. Megan ran over and gave her a hug, and mentioned she had seen her class perform at Sandi's on Thursday.

Wearing jeans, tennis shoes, a black leather jacket, and his signature freedom hat, Cicero arrived at seven o'clock. Megan jumped up and led the audience in a standing ovation.

Cicero waved at a room filled with old to the very young in blue jeans, various colored work pants, and a skirt here and there. There were baseball and stocking caps with logos, and a few cowboy hats. What he noticed most was the anxious working-class smiles.

Cicero faced his audience. "Tonight we're going to have a conversation about courage and its importance to society and good government. Raise your hand if you have questions or comments."

Cicero grabbed a cup of coffee, and said, "Aristotle defined courage as a moral virtue measured between extremes like cowardice and excessive confidence. A courageous person doesn't fear the powerful, harmful things, or even death in the right cause. A coward would avoid those risks, while the over confident recklessly takes on risk and for the wrong reasons. Wrong reasons would include personal glory or personal wealth enhancement. For Aristotle, the end of your courageous action must be some good or worthwhile cause for the community—sacrifice for the good of others. Courage is noble because it contributes to the well-being of the community. You have a memorial near the courthouse that honors those who gave their all in past conflicts—that's what courage is all about. That memorial testifies to the courage we had in us back in those days."

An elderly woman holding a young child stood. "We're not at war with anybody now. Do we still need courage?"

"Society needs the courageous because threats to our freedom and good government never go away."

Megan raised her hand. "Tell us about these threats."

Cicero glanced around the room. "How many of you have heard of the term Deep State?"

Most of the audience raised their hands.

A young man wearing an orange stocking cap shouted from the back row. "My history teacher said that's urban myth stuff concocted by the far right."

Cicero smiled. "What do you think?"

"I don't know."

Megan jumped up and faced the young man. "It exists and it doesn't tolerate dissent. Your dumb-ass teacher doesn't know shit. Cicero will put you straight."

Cicero saluted Megan. "I'll do my best."

Cicero refilled his cup, and then continued. "Like all totalitarian movements, the Deep State relies on hate, intimidation, and even violence to smash dissent. Anyone having the wrong kind of thinking is deemed a threat to their growing political, economic, and cultural hold on power. When threatened, many people lack the courage to stand up to the Deep State. But courage is the only way to overcome this challenge to the America we know—or knew.

"The Deep State is well organized and driven by an arrogant, self-righteous lust for power and wealth. It consists of high-level government bureaucrats at the Justice and State Departments, the Federal Judiciary, and of course the IRS. It also includes moneyed globalists, politicians and people in media and academia. Hell, someone in this room might be working for the Deep State.

"Look, totalitarian evil has been with us forever. Aristotle thought about it over two-thousand years ago, and supplied the remedy—moral courage. The twentieth century was filled with challenge from Fascists on the right to Communists on the left, and our fathers and grandfathers demonstrated the moral courage to defeat those totalitarian threats. We need that same level of commitment today."

As rain began to pelt the twenty-five foot high metal roof, Mrs. Nifong's husband stood. "What can we do?"

"Work for the common good. Step out of the shadows and demand truth from government, media, academia, and other powerful institutions. Point out bias and corruption wherever you perceive it. Know when you're being bamboozled, and take nothing for granted. Be polite but forceful. Refuse to go away when they push back."

"What are the risks?"

"Totalitarian movements need acquiescent citizenry. They know there's always a few troublemakers, but the few can't become too many or their grip on power will be challenged. If the Deep State sees you as a threat it will come after you, and has a lot of ways to do it. If it doesn't like what you're writing, you won't find a publisher or an outlet for your work. Remember a couple of months back when that well-known entertainer Johnny Karl had to keep running to microphones to apologize, apologize, and apologize for saying something the totalitarians didn't like. Hell, they almost got his top rated TV show canceled. They attack your right to earn. Radio talk show guys are always having their sponsors threatened. Teachers know they can get forced out for expressing opinions not in line with Deep State thinking. The Deep State also intimidates by sending hate mobs to people's homes, or when they're having dinner at a restaurant, or to a classroom.

"Last year out in California a hate mob invaded a history instructor's classroom and demanded she resign because she had suggested the Deep State was real and dangerous. That story never got reported by mainstream media, but the incident was recorded by a student and it's out there on social media. Go watch those thugs push poor Carol Smith against the blackboard and slap her around—nobody came to her aid. The university let Carol go at the end of the semester. And that was that."

Cicero paused a moment, and then said, "Pardon my language, but anything can happen if they can't make you shut the fuck up."

A woman yelled, "You think they do murder?"

"I'm convinced they do. There have been too many so-called suicides, accidents, and disappearances of Deep State critics. A couple of years ago Larry Guzman, a journalist friend of mine, wrote a series of articles exposing lies and brutality of Deep State bureaucrats, politicians, and agencies like the FBI. Since then no one has seen or heard from him. They do whatever it takes to get and keep power."

The woman nodded. "Aren't you afraid you might be targeted?"

Cicero took off his cap and ran his hand through his wavy gray hair. "I'm cautious, but not afraid."

Over the next two hours Cicero shared details of his personal background including what led him to embark on his courage crusade. Mrs. Nifong rose several times and demanded more courageous action from those in the room. A beautician named Dianne committed to building a freedom blog. And teenagers in the back said they would challenge their teachers whenever they made a wacko comment in class.

A little after nine, Cicero glanced up as the wind and rain began to rattle the metal roof.

He finished his coffee, and said, "So where do we go from here? I'll continue communicating the importance of freedom and courage. If you haven't already, read Aristotle on ethics and politics, and Orwell's *1984*. That's wisdom for the ages. Where you go will be yours and the country's business. But, I urge you to approach this challenge with a sense of urgency. The Deep State and its allies are on the march."

Cicero thanked everyone for coming, many promised to read the books, and a few committed to courageous action. A couple of teenagers scooped up the remaining candy.

Megan waited till most had left, and then pulled Cicero aside. "What you said was so important and right on. This week I've experienced the good and evil out there, and you've convinced me good is worth fighting for regardless of the risks."

Cicero began to smile, but Megan held up her hand. "I have a confession to make. For the past ten years I've been on the payroll of the Deep State, and the past week I've been spying on you."

Cicero stared a moment, and then put his hands on Megan's shoulders. "It took a lot of courage to tell me that."

Megan wiped a tear. "There's more. The Deep State wants you dead. I'm supposed to set you up tonight. There's a monster named Red waiting for my phone call to let him know when you head back to your motel. He and his lunatic gang are going to grab you, load you up with drugs, and send you and your car over a cliff or down a ravine. I won't be a part of that."

"Megan, we can't be intimated by these thugs. I have to continue what I'm doing—freedom is not disposable."

She handed Cicero his jacket. "There are killers out there expecting a call from me. Dammit, you're alone and won't have a chance if they catch up with you tonight. Get the hell out and survive to fight another day."

Cicero started to put on his jacket, and then paused. "OK, I'll head to O'Fallon. I have friends and supporters there."

Around nine-thirty, they hurried to Cicero's car in the pouring rain, checking around the dark empty parking lot as they went.

He rolled down the window and grabbed Megan's hand. "I'm not leaving until I know you'll be safe. Do you have a place to go?"

"I'll be fine. I've already packed clothes and personal items in my car. I'm driving straight to Little Rock. I know a lot of stuff about the Deep State I need to share with you. I'll reach out when I think it's safe. For now I'll disappear—they won't find me."

With her blond hair soaked and rain rolling down her face, Megan leaned over and kissed Cicero. "I wish we had met ten years ago."

As Cicero's car splashed through several large puddles and pulled onto the main road, Megan smiled and walked slowly to her car.

About the Author

Hourston's other works of fiction include:

Monsters on Trial
What happens when America grants its mad, bad monsters legal rights? The answer is found in nine exciting short stories where Mike Hoffmann and his team battle vampires, werewolves, zombies, and other goblins—mostly in court. This book is available at Amazon in paperback and e-Book. It's also available at Barnes and Noble, and Kobo as an e-Book.

R.I.P. When All is Said and Done
A collection of five exciting stories that explore the meaning of justice, the afterlife, revenge, days gone by, and a poet's world. Available in paperback and e-Book at Amazon. It's also available at Barnes and Noble, and Kobo as an e-Book.

Hourston has master degrees in history (MA) and business administration (MBA) from the University of Missouri-St. Louis.